Teachers in Control

Teachers in Control

Cracking the Code

Martin Powell and Jonathan Solity

London and New York

First published 1990 by Routledge
11 New Fetter Lane, London EC4P 4EE

Simultaneously published in the USA and Canada
by Routledge
a division of Routledge, Chapman and Hall, Inc.
29 West 35th Street, New York, NY 10001

Typeset by LaserScript Ltd, Mitcham, Surrey
Printed and bound in Great Britain by
Biddles Ltd, Guildford and King's Lynn

British Library Cataloguing in Publication Data

Powell, Martin
   Teachers in control, cracking the code.
   1. Great Britain. Teaching
I. Title II. Solity, Jonathan
371.1020941
ISBN 0-415-04885-0

Library of Congress Cataloging-in-Publication Data

Powell, Martin
   Teachers in control: cracking the code/
Martin Powell, Jonathan Solity.
      p.   cm.
   Includes bibliographical references.
   ISBN 0-415-04885-0—ISBN 0-415-03668-2 (pbk.)
   1. Teachers—Attitudes. 2. Teaching—Decision making.
3. Teaching, Freedom of. I. Solity, Jonathan. II. Title.
LB1775.S63 1990
371.1—dc20   89-71070
                                                     CIP

This book is dedicated to Sue and Anna,
and to the memory of Tom,
from whom I have learned so much.

Jonathan Solity

Contents

Acknowledgements

In writing this book we have very much appreciated the helpful comments and advice received from Sue Clark, Professor John Eggleston, Derek Pope, and Pat Sikes. Special thanks go to our partners, Gwen and Sue, for their patience and support while the book was being prepared. Although we acknowledge, with gratitude, the influence of others on our thinking, the views expressed in this book are ours and do not necessarily reflect the views of our employers – Birmingham City Council and the University of Warwick.

Chapter One

Introduction: Cracking the code

A teacher sits at her desk in the classroom one afternoon, after all the children have gone home. In front of her are a pile of mathematics books. Behind her, on the wall, is a schematic plan of the maths project that the children have been tackling, involving petrol consumption figures for cars. On the plan, she and other colleagues have listed the specific attainment targets in the National Curriculum and some steps that lead to these targets. As she glances at some of the children's work, she thinks about the wide disparity of skill levels among the children and how she needs to find better ways of checking whether they have the necessary skills for each part of the project. This is a departmental project so she will also need to discuss her ideas with the other teachers in the project team. She wishes that it had a subject content that appealed more to the girls, although she and the other teachers in her department are thinking about how to balance the mathematical content in terms of gender interest.

It has not been a bad lesson. Just a couple of the children had found it difficult to understand what to do. She had paired them with more able children and that had seemed to work, but was that really fair on those more able children? She wasn't sure. What had really annoyed her was the way that Jody had messed about. He is quite able verbally, but like a number of the children in the class, when it comes to reading and comprehending mathematical information embedded in a problem, he finds it hard-going and plays up. Often he plays up even when he can manage the work. She really must talk to the head of year about him, he seems to be getting worse. She had felt herself getting really angry with him. He always manages to appear really insolent in the slow way he does everything and the challenging looks he gives her. Now, as she thinks about the lesson, her memories of it tend to be tinged with annoyance about Jody.

She collects the books together to take them home with her tonight. Now it's time for a whole staff meeting to look at the work she and a couple of others have been doing on school rules as part of the school's approach to discipline. Both the school's adviser and the psychologist are going to be there. It's going to be another late night. At least some of the rush-hour traffic will have gone by the time she goes home. She remembers that she needs to do some late-night shopping on the way home or there will be nothing for her meal.

This scene is imaginary, but, we hope, not so fanciful that you will not identify with some parts of it. We have begun in this way in order to illustrate that the issues that concern us in education are not unusual or out of the ordinary. What our scene depicts is a conscientious teacher making sense of her job. She is trying to find ways of coping with the considerable demands on her time and still give of her best within the classroom.

The scene depicts the teacher neither totally in control of all the events in her professional life nor totally unable to control events. She is performing a balancing act. On the one side of the fulcrum are all the external pressures and demands on her; on the other side are her personal skills, ability to organize herself, and commitment. Our experience in talking to teachers and watching them working in schools is that this balance is maintained with extreme difficulty. Teachers find themselves not having the time or energy to step back and think about how to deal with the very problem of not having time for planning. Problems without solutions become sources of stress to teachers.

One view of teachers in such circumstances is to see them spread along a line. At the one end of the line are the teachers who feel totally powerless: they feel they have no means to influence what happens to them professionally. At the other end of the line are teachers who feel totally in control of their work and their professional lives. Most teachers are at some point along the line between these two extremes. In our experience, external pressures on teachers tend to force them further down the line towards the powerless end.

We wanted to write a book that might be of help to teachers to counter some of the external pressures, so that, while not being independent of influence, teachers would feel able to manage their own decisions. This has been our intention, but our approach to how we might do it has changed as we have gone along. This chapter outlines the content of the book and introduces some of the themes that run through it related to combating feelings of powerlessness. Before going on to look at those themes directly, it may be useful to spend a little time examining how the book came to take its current shape.

When we came together to plan this book, we had a couple of major themes that we wished to pursue to help teachers gain the necessary evidence upon which to base their decisions. We felt that one useful approach to evidence in the classroom was through behavioural psychology. We were aware, however, that such an approach was not universally popular in education. We had visions of producing for teachers an account of behavioural psychology that emphasized its ethical virtues. This reflected our opinion that behavioural psychology had been much maligned in the educational literature. Our second theme was concerned with the way decisions were made. It seemed to us, at least, that in education at a national, local, school, and classroom level, decisions were being made that were not based on evidence. As psychologists, we took the view then that the careful collection, presentation, and consideration of data was the only way to approach decision making. It will not take you long, as you read this book, to realize that our views have changed considerably.

We still believe that behavioural psychology has had an unfortunate press. In many ways, the emphasis within behavioural psychology on the observable and the measurable makes it more open and less inclined to inference than other types of psychology. Its practitioners have taken to negotiating contracts with clients that rely less on interpretation and analysis than do other branches of psychotherapy. Moreover, both in its clinical application with children and families, and its curricular application in terms of measurable products of learning, behavioural psychology has had substantial impact. We shall argue in later chapters that its proponents and opponents, particularly in relation to the curriculum, often have more in common than their initial stances might suggest. Despite rising here to the defence of behavioural approaches, however, we have forsaken any claim to be exclusively based within that camp.

As regards our other theme, we no longer argue that decisions made in education that are based on evidence will be the solution to all our problems. Our position has become more complicated. We have come round to viewing evidence, like beauty, to be in the eye of the beholder. Whereas, at first, we thought that teachers only needed access to evidence to be able to make good decisions in the classroom, we began to realize that life was more complicated than that. Evidence is not neutral, it is selected and interpreted. We began to take the view that each of us has a singular view of the world and that some part of our energies in social interaction is taken up with trying to influence other people's views – just as we are doing now! This made us realize that teachers are subjected to enormous influence on their professional work from all directions. Our experience as psychologists has given us a particular position from which to view the process of influence, since, in no small measure, our job too involved attempting to affect how teachers work.

At first, we thought that one of the best ways of helping teachers to sort out all these influences on their work would be to explore ways of helping teachers to collect evidence that would contribute to better classroom problem solving. As we began to think about how to help teachers deal with and sort through all this influence bearing down on their practice, however, we uncovered a key theme to do with values. We came to the view that influences on teachers are by no means always obvious. While much energy is spent on trying to influence the views of others, a great deal of energy is spent on hiding one's own views, and, more critically, the values and other factors that underpin them.

As well as face-to-face influences, arising from people with whom teachers come into contact as part of their job, we also recognized that our model of influence needed to extend into organizational factors and societal factors. We looked at how key elements interrelate in the organization of education in our society and at how they shape classroom practice. We began to ask questions about the values that are implied or contained in the way these elements control education in the classroom. As we did so, we realized that we also needed to explore personal values and influences on the individual. Educational administration, inspection, and advice are undertaken by people who have been attracted by aspects of such work. What attracts some people and not others? What attracts teachers to teaching? These are questions which direct us towards looking for ways of understanding individuals.

No doubt all writers on educational matters have the same thoughts about their timing, whenever they happen to be writing, but we think this has been a particularly difficult time to choose to write a book about factors that affect the way that teachers work. With so many changes emanating from the 1988 Education Reform Act and the ensuing Orders and Regulations, it has been hard to sift out the transient from the permanent. Attempting to map the major structural elements of the educational system as they break away from their moorings and float away on the outgoing tide has not been easy. Moreover, we have seen at this time a teaching profession 'punch-drunk' not only by the changes but also by the rate of change.

Our initial purpose in writing this book was to help teachers to have more say in the professional decisions about practice in the classroom. Now we are even more convinced of the need for this. A balance has to be struck, of course, between teacher autonomy and teacher accountability. No one will be happy at the prospect of individual teachers operating as mavericks within their own classrooms, with the door shut, totally impervious to outside influence. It seems to us, however, that with the National Curriculum, pupil profiling, and assessment and teacher appraisal, the scope for such individualism has been substantially reduced; we think, on the whole, that is a change for the better. On the other hand, teachers, already open to the undue influence of outside experts, have now to operate within a more imposed system. The curriculum seems to have been packaged and presented to teachers, and there is a danger that their own wisdom and expertise will be diminished by that process. As you progress through this book, you will see that we believe that the imposed changes have by no means removed the need for using imagination and inventiveness, for developing teaching methods and theories about the processes of education itself. Because teachers may have been pushed further down the line towards power-lessness and because some measure of independence is still very much needed, we would like to find ways of helping teachers to establish a basis for validating and having confidence in their own decisions.

We have said that we see scope for many aspects of work to remain very much within teacher control. But if teachers lose confidence in their own powers to make decisions and in the acceptability of their decisions to parents, governors, and others who judge their worth, then there are bound to be problems. The classroom is a dynamic setting with a huge number of social interactions, bits of information to be mentally processed, and decisions to be made by the teacher every few seconds. Any damage to the teacher's confidence to do the job would substan-tially interfere with effective teaching.

The Education Reform Act has had enormous influence on teachers and teaching. Whatever its merits and faults, there is a danger that its imposition, although providing a framework in which to operate, will have reduced the level of teacher initiative. Our view is that with a determination to examine the sources and nature of influences on their practice, teachers are in better shape to make accountable decisions in which they, and others, may have confidence.

This book seeks to help teachers to develop a means of analysing the influences on their practice – a means, if you like, of cracking the code. We don't provide the cypher that simply enables the code to be broken: if only life were so simple. We shall have succeeded in our aim if we have encouraged you to assume a more critical perspective towards educational practice and the theories and evidence on which it is based, or not based as the case may be. We also hope we will have encouraged you to continue the long journey of self-understanding, and to undertake the more immediate task of finding out who you are in relation to teaching. This is not a comfortable process, nor do we think this book is comforting. We do take a positive view, none the less, especially regard-ing the way that we might move towards resolving the differences that stem from the unique views all of us have on life.

One part of resolving the interpersonal differences that can bedevil co-operative progress depends on greater openness about our values and a willingness to negotiate with others. In advocating a willingness to negotiate, we are not suggesting that we should all abandon our funda-mental values, but that we should be prepared to hear what others are saying and should actively seek common ground if possible. We explore some of the factors that might stand in the way of our negotiating with others, with the view that such self-knowledge can help us overcome our own barriers.

Being willing to declare your values is not a comfortable exercise and we discuss the implications of doing so in a later chapter. *Our* values include the view that keeping hidden the purposes behind attempts to influence the behaviour of others is a form of manipulation. Our concern about the way in which teachers are subjected to pressures and influence from so many quarters is not only the stress this puts teachers under, but also the limited extent to which these influences are open, understand-able, and non-manipulative. Influence need not be manipulative, but, whatever the moral value of the ends it promotes, if it hides its purpose and steals up on folk, then it *is* manipulative. In their book, *Teaching as a Subversive Activity*, Postman and Weingartner (1969) stress the need for schools to become centres for 'crap-detection'. In their view, human survival, no less, requires students to acquire from their education a capacity for intelligent resistance to propaganda, a point we shall consider in a later chapter. It is unlikely that students will acquire this resistance to propaganda unless their teachers have done the same.

We see influence as an integral part of social interaction, and, as we have already acknowledged, it is a process that we are using at this very moment. Manipulation and openness are at opposite ends of a dimension that we can use to describe influence. We should like to think that we are trying to influence you in an open way. (We should also like to think that you will feel more able to make up your own mind about that, once you have read this book!) Manipulative influence can take many forms and can be dressed up in the most respectable and persuasive language. One way of presenting arguments and evidence that reduces the vigilance of 'crap-detectors' is to adopt the form and language of science. We seek to alert teachers to some of the implications of such neutral sounding words as 'evidence', 'facts', 'knowledge', and 'truth'. Bronowski (1960) in *The Common Sense of Science*, reminds us of the need to use these terms with care. He states:

> [Truth] is common to all systems of value, and is fundamental to most of them, and it is a value. We cannot take it for granted as something self-evident in science any more than in art or morals or religion. In all of them truth rests on an act of free human judgement. In none of them of course can this judgement be exercised without experience: there is no truth, not even religious truth, which calls for no sanction from fact. There are other values: goodness, beauty, right conduct. They have their echoes even in science; and there is one value, freedom of human ideas, which is the essential condition for the health of science.

Because we recognize the seductive dangers of arguments and evidence presented as science, we spend some time discussing the importance of values that underpin science. We also look at the need for care in how language is used. Attempts to analyse influence and to counter manipulation require careful attention to the use of language. We spend time considering the implications of this for interpersonal communication as well as for countering propaganda. To help you counter *our* propaganda, it might be helpful if we said a little more about our values. This will give you more of a context in which to consider the views we present.

In brief, we are committed to free state education, which strives to offer equal opportunities to all and actively seeks to eliminate discriminatory practices, particularly those based on gender, social class, ethnicity, and ability. We are also committed to educating children in such a way that they learn to accept responsibility for their actions, to think critically and independently, and to become active participants in negotiating the nature of their learning experiences.

We also, in a paradoxical way, believe in doubt. We consider that uncertainty is the only tenable stance in facing the unknown. Uncertainty and doubt are not negative characteristics, however, since on them is based a true acceptance of the right of others to hold a different point of view. Our paradox is that we are certain about doubt and doubtful about certainty. Of course there are some aspects of our experience that we hold with certainty. At least, our experience has taught us to act as if we were certain that fire burns and ice freezes. But as we move from the tangible and observable towards the interpretative and thoughtful, we become less certain.

Another of our values is that since much of what we know belongs to each of us as private experiences, it behoves us to negotiate our knowledge with others and not impose it. We discuss later in the book some ways we can get over the problem of not having common experience. It follows from these values that we see children as people with rights, having an entitlement to a view of their world. According status to children's views and negotiating rather than imposing knowledge, in our view, enables adults to model the behaviour that we are advocating and helps children to progress towards that behaviour.

The book is in four parts. In Part I, we identify some of the main elements of the education system that exert influence within that system. We also look at what it is that people most seek to control in education, namely the curriculum. We conclude the section by looking at some of the issues that surround the curriculum and the way those issues are presented. We also look at how views are promoted or discredited and the likely impact this has on teachers.

Part II begins with a look at how organizations promote collective values and how these influence the individual. We also look at individual values and how these are often hidden. Chapter Six looks at the way that practices in education can be sustained by social processes such as myths, rather than by more recognizable theoretical justifications. Chapter Seven then looks at how language can reveal underlying values and how it can be used to manipulate.

Part III addresses some psychological factors that shape the lives, behaviour, and career choice of teachers and, ultimately, the pattern of interaction with children. We look at the work of psychologists who argue that many of these influential factors operate without our being aware of their impact on us and, in the case of teachers, on our educational practice. We examine the role of psychology in education in Chapter Eight, and the way it is usually introduced to teachers. Then, in Chapter Nine, we look at a particular model of how people make sense of their world and how this might apply to teachers in their work.

In Chapter Ten, the role of early upbringing and family life is looked at, not just as a way of understanding the children with whom we work, but as contributing to an understanding of ourselves. Consideration is given to how we might escape the psychological straitjacket that shapes our thinking and behaviour and which can control our interactions as teachers in the classroom and with colleagues in the staffroom. We end Part III by highlighting what we see to be key areas to be taken into account as we seek to engage in the sort of straight and open communication that we believe is essential.

Part IV is a single chapter, Chapter Twelve, which presents a view about the personal and professional qualities we appear to be promoting. If you move towards adopting an approach to evidence, towards a deeper understanding of yourself as a person, and towards the negotiation of what you know and believe, what sort of teacher and what sort of a person are you? We believe that you will at least have begun the process of 'cracking your own code'.

Part I

In Part I we wish to convey a sense of the overall scenario in which teachers now have to work. We familiarize readers with some of the major elements that make up the education system and exert influence on schools and teachers. We then look at three areas of school life – what is taught, teaching style, and evaluating children's learning – to illustrate how values underpin practice in each area, and how, despite the imposition of the National Curriculum, there is scope for teachers to evolve their practice in ways that accord with their own values. We suggest that there is still much that teachers can influence. We conclude Part I by looking at the psychological influences on educational practice. We examine the way the debate takes place as well as the respective merits of different theories of teaching and learning.

Chapter Two

Controlling education

We have three aims in this chapter. First we seek to familiarize readers with some of the major elements that make up the education system and exert influence on the school and teachers in the classroom. Our perspective encourages the reader to adopt a healthily sceptical view about the extent to which straightforward factual descriptions can portray the values of some of these elements.

Second we wish to provide a brief introduction to the context in which schools and teachers are now required to function. Our overall concerns in this book are with the influences on teachers' everyday educational practice, and how teachers might be encouraged to cast a critical eye towards those that seek to promote particular ideologies or styles of teaching. Prior to this we wish to convey a sense of the wider developing educational scene to set the context for our discussion on the areas that teachers themselves still have considerable power to influence.

A third aim relates to a theme we develop throughout this book: that things are not always as they seem. Different organizations and institutions are involved in education for all sorts of reasons. Some of these reasons are clear and probably undisputed. They will be reflected in rhetoric about improving standards, providing choice, and developing children's potential. Other reasons are much more likely to remain concealed and hidden from public view.

We mentioned in Chapter One that people's values are rarely declared in educational debate, that language may be used to manipulate rather than to aid communications, and that personal motives for action are hidden behind the rhetoric of scientific debate. What people do not wish to bring into the open for discussion remains metaphorically behind a screen, unavailable for public scrutiny. Our intention therefore, is to begin to look behind 'the screen' of those involved in education. We wish to examine the relationships between them and offer some speculative and tentative interpretations on their roles and contribution to the education system.

Who is involved in the field of education?

The figure below summarizes the way in which we group together the elements that make up the education system. For the sake of descriptive clarity, we have arranged the elements into three major headings – central and local government; educational organizations and institutions; and schools – and have assumed some similarities among the elements that we have put together. In addition, however, it has to be recognized that there will be connections across these groupings.

Some elements of the education system

CENTRAL AND LOCAL GOVERNMENT	
central government	**local government**
Members of Parliament DES HMI	LEA officers local councillors advisers/inspectors

EDUCATIONAL ORGANIZATIONS AND INSTITUTIONS
university/polytechnic education departments research/evaluation/testing agencies publishers teacher unions vountary associations and pressure groups the media

SCHOOL INFLUENCES
community governors parents teachers children

The whole system is enormously complex and analysis is not assisted by the fact that the product of the educational system is not easily defined. We shall discuss this point at greater length in the next chapter, but suffice it to say here that it is very difficult to determine the influence that individual elements exert on each other and on the system as a whole and that the process necessarily remains speculative and subject to qualification.

Central and local government are the elements of the system which serve the electorate and are politically accountable. Educational organizations and institutions exert influence through the control of information in the training of teachers, through research, and through publishing books and materials. Teacher unions, although elected (by their members), are not accountable to the general public and yet have influence that extends beyond the individual school. The opinion-makers of the media, the voluntary associations, and pressure groups also belong in this box. The third box represents the school and the community that it serves.

These neat boxes are useful for diagrammatic and descriptive purposes, but life is not so readily compartmentalized. It might seem that the elements described have corporate views, that we can talk about the aims of a particular local education authority, school, university, or polytechnic education department. However, in doing so, we need to bear in mind that we may well be concealing a range of attitudes and opinions held by the individuals working within those groups who do not necessarily support 'company policy'.

We have briefly said who makes up the education system. We would now like to say a little about how it functions and exerts influence on educational practice. In so doing we look at the relationship between central and local government and schools. We also discuss what we perceive to be, in part, the motivation for the involvement of the various educational organizations and institutions within the system that we have identified. Finally, we draw attention to the area where we feel teachers can exercise considerable control and autonomy – the curriculum – but we reserve detailed discussion on this topic for Chapters Three and Four.

A framework for practice

Typically, central and local government have worked in partnership to provide a framework and context in which education takes place. The partnership has always generated tension, especially where different political parties have been responsible for different levels of government. The relationship between the two cannot be viewed as static, but as being in a state of continuous change, punctuated from time to time by legislation reflecting how the different roles are emerging.

Central government

Central government comprises three groups: Members of Parliament, the Department of Education and Science, and Her Majesty's Inspector-ate. They come to the world of education with very different levels of expertise and experience in educational matters. What they might advo-cate is also underpinned by differing values, beliefs, and motivations.

Members of Parliament are, of course, drawn from a wide range of trades and professions, with individuals not necessarily having any recent direct experience of education. None the less, a quick thumb through the biographies of Members suggests that quite a number are ex-teachers or ex-lecturers. When invited to indicate their areas of particular interest in Dod's Parliamentary Companion (1988), 123 MPs listed education as an interest, the most common area of interest after trade and industry and foreign affairs. Irrespective of their previous background, interest, and experience of the education system, politicians enter the political arena with their own well-established opinions about education. The political world of MPs demands this of them and their views are therefore based on their party political loyalties. What can often be confusing is that stated educational aims and outcomes for children voiced by politicians on the political left and right might sound similar, but the means for achieving them are very different.

The DES represents the administrative arm of central government. These are the civil servants who advise on, and assist in, the drafting of legislation. Although it cannot be assumed that they have had any teaching experience, they can be viewed as professional educationalists in that they spend a considerable part of their working life within the civil service at the DES and so may well acquire considerable experience in educational matters. Whereas governments and their ministers may come and go, DES staff can be seen as providing continuity.

The DES establishes the legal framework within which local authorities and schools operate. Some laws, including the Education Reform Act, not only specify what must happen, but also create the space for the Secretary of State for Education and Science to introduce Regulations and Orders that spell out the details at a later date. The DES also lays down a framework for funding all levels of education. Of immediate concern to schools is the framework for the devolution of financial management from the LEA to schools, established under the 1988 Education Act. The implications for the role of the LEA will be mentioned later, but the DES has the responsibility of approving the local formula for delegating financial control to schools or for providing a formula, where the LEA has failed to do so satisfactorily.

The DES is a potent, albeit somewhat distant, force in the world of education. Through its control of the purse strings, it can exert a considerable influence on the education children receive.

Who advises the government on educational matters?

The third strand to central government is Her Majesty's Inspectorate who provide the professional input into policy making and the drafting of legislation. The Inspectorate differs from the other two elements in at least one important way. Whereas it is not necessary for MPs, the Secretary of State for Education and Science, or civil servants working in the DES to have teaching experience, all HMI are required to have taught and the majority can be assumed to have had considerable teaching experience, usually in senior positions in schools. However, there are indications that this requirement is changing. An advert for HMI which appeared in *The Times Educational Supplement* on 12 May 1989 stated: 'applicants are usually aged between 35 and 45 with experience drawn from successful careers in education but also, increasingly, from commerce and industry'.

Within central government, HMI have been viewed as an independent group of professional educators, who advise, but are not controlled by, the government. According to Lawton and Gordon (1987), 'the essential role of HMI is to advise the Secretary of State for Education and his department' (Lawton and Gordon, 1987:4). They advise on policy making together with more general educational issues. Although Lawton and Gordon feel that the autonomy of HMI is one way of restraining the activities of politicians and civil servants, there are those who would argue that the independence of the Inspectorate has been compromised.

We suspect that many people working in education today might view HMI as one of the most powerful groups of professional educationalists (as against politicians or civil servants) in the system – possibly as the most powerful. Although perhaps lacking the individual power of Chief Education Officers within LEAs, they are collectively more cohesive at a national level. Moreover, they have certain legally defined powers of inspection of all state-maintained educational establishments and the duty to make their reports publicly available. As well as reporting on individual schools and colleges, the Inspectorate draws together themes from such reports to issue guidelines on good practice, in areas as diverse as styles of teaching, curriculum development, pastoral work, and the design of buildings. This power to inspect, advise, and set out guidelines on 'good practice' puts HMI in a position of some authority within education.

Our own concerns about the independence of the Inspectorate derive from the fact that all their reports are credited to HMI in general rather than to those particular individuals who are responsible for compiling them. This implies a willingness to adhere to 'company policy'. Whilst this protects individuals from criticism, as no single HMI is identified as expressing critical, negative, and generally unpopular opinions, it begs the question of how far individual perceptions are tailored to conform to the corporate view.

As civil servants, HMI forgo the freedom to write articles and books about education, except within the framework of their official reports. They are not entitled to air their personal opinions on education except as members of the Inspectorate. We are of course aware that many people, within and outside education, have to give up a measure of personal independence for the sake of company or corporate loyalty.

One issue is to do with the trade-off between power and independence of view.

In the light of this issue, it is reasonable to ask what sort of person is attracted to the exercise of power, especially that which demands the sacrifice of an independent opinion for the sake of a collegiate one. For us there is a serious question as to whether people who are willing to conform are able to maintain an independence of view. This question is particularly apposite at a time of general awareness of a shift in the balance of power away from the civil servants in the DES towards the politicians in the government. Perhaps now, more than ever, there is a need for advisers who refuse to toe the line, whose views cannot be sanitized, and who challenge the orthodoxies of DES and government alike.

Alternative sources of advice   The DES also seeks formal advice from alternative sources to HMI through the reports they commission. From time to time Secretaries of State have commissioned reports from advisory bodies concerning specific aspects of education. Some of these have reported on the findings of working parties set up to investigate various aspects of educational practice. They have frequently become associated with the name of the person chairing the working party (e.g. the Plowden, Bullock, Warnock, and Elton Reports).

The influence of pressure groups   Our discussion so far has described the formal structure of central government but there are other influences, independent of the DES and HMI, on the policies pursued by any government: these come from pressure groups which campaign at local and national levels. An early example of their impact occurred in the 1960s.

In the period around the publication of the Plowden Report (CACE 1967), so-called 'progressive' education was at its height. In 1969, the first Black Papers (Cox and Dyson 1969a, 1969b) were published, openly criticizing such educational philosophy. The contributors to these papers could be seen to be writing from an overtly political stance unsympathetic to the ideology embodied in Plowden. It is not possible to estimate the impact that these authors had, but they certainly provided a powerful lobby against much educational practice that was being welcomed and advocated at the time.

There followed, in 1974, the William Tyndale School affair, where a school seen to be implementing progressive methods came under severe critical scrutiny. The outcomes at this school were seen to be illustrative of what could happen if progressive methods were allowed to be implemented without restraint. William Tyndale grew from a local issue concerning teachers, parents, and the LEA to become a national political one.

16

These developments have their parallels today in terms of the groups that have the ear of the government. The Centre for Policy Studies was established in 1974 by Sir Keith Joseph and Mrs Margaret Thatcher, to provide what Maclure describes as 'a focus for new Right Thinking and the confident expression of hitherto unfashionable views' (1988:153). Maclure identifies other right-wing educational pressure groups, including the Campaign for Real Education, the National Grammar School Association, Parental Alliance for Choice in Education, and Parents for English Education Rights. He suggests that such groups have brought previously less than acceptable views into common currency and helped change the boundaries of educational debate. Perhaps the fact that the government seeks alternative sources of advice is an indication that HMI is still seen to be able to offer impartial advice. At the same time, however, it might indicate that the Prime Minister wants advice from outside the DES in order to remove the initiative from the DES.

Our comments relate very much to the activities of successive Conservative governments elected between 1979 and 1987. However, were the government of the day of a different political persuasion, there is every reason to believe that it too would have advisory groups, conducting research and helping to formulate policy with political leanings sympathetic to itself.

Let us summarize what we have been saying about central government. It comprises three groups: politicians, officials in the DES, and professional educationalists in the shape of HMI. In our introduction to this chapter we indicated that individual values are rarely aired publicly and thus placed on the agenda for discussion and debate. In the context of central government, only politicians are expected and permitted to declare their values, and then only within the boundaries of their party. Officials and Inspectors are expected to have values wholly consistent with the execution of their official duties.

In some senses, it is possible to be much clearer about the values and attitudes of politicians than of either administrators or HMI. Politicians achieve a position of influence only after declaring their values – albeit only some of their values – and submitting themselves to the electorate to decide whether those views should be advanced in Parliament. Civil servants, including HMI, on the other hand, operate behind an ostensible screen of impartiality and detachment. They are seen to be non-political and would claim, perhaps, to be influenced only by professional concerns. The extent to which decisions can really be administrative or educational, rather than political or influenced by personal factors, is debatable and one we shall be examining closely in later chapters.

Local government

Local government, like central government, comprises a number of different departments, one of which is education. LEAs can be seen to mirror, at the local level, the functions of central government. This is also true of their patterns of organization to the extent that they, also, incorporate political, administrative, and professional elements, in the way we have described for central government.

The Education Department that serves the LEA is staffed by administrators, who advise the Education Committee and have the responsibility for implementing committee policy. The role of LEAs has been drastically changed by the 1988 Education Reform Act. Many of their powers have been stripped and diverted to central government or schools. The function of LEAs in the future will be on the one hand to ensure schools meet their obligations under the Act, and on the other to support them in doing so.

The role of LEA administrators can be seen to parallel that of civil servants at the DES. They must take account of the legal responsibilities and duties of the LEA and interpret central government legislation and regulations. They are responsible to politicians, in this case locally elected councillors, and usually work closely with inspectors, who at the local level have some common ground with HMI.

Inspectors, called advisers in some local authorities, in turn become a direct link between administrators and schools. They are regarded as being successful classroom practitioners of some experience and in the past have generally advised on aspects of good practice. They have also helped to develop policy locally as well as to implement policy decisions made within the LEA and at national level. In the future it is likely they will be helping schools to implement the National Curriculum, while at the same time playing a key role in quality control, ensuring schools achieve acceptable standards. They will probably also be involved in schemes of teacher appraisal. Certainly they have a major role to play in the future although it cannot be assumed that they will continue to be financed directly by LEAs, under the new funding arrangements introduced by the Education Reform Act.

Central and local government provide the legal, financial, and educational framework in which others involved in the field of education operate. In the discussion that follows we look at the means by which influence is potentially brought to bear on educational practice by educational organizations and institutions.

Influences on educational practice

It is difficult to identify how the educational organizations and institutions identified in Figure 2.1 actually influence the teaching and learning processes. We can at best only speculate on their likely impact on teachers and the context in which they operate. Any influence they might bring to bear has to be set alongside the personal factors that shape individual teaching styles and the financial constraints that so often limit the realization of teachers' aims.

Does higher education influence education practice?

An intending teacher's first formal contact with his or her future role comes through attending an approved course of initial teacher education (although in the future alternative avenues will offer entry into the profession). Unfortunately there has been little research to suggest that teacher education courses exert the powerful influence which might be anticipated, given that they occur at a time when students are likely to be most receptive to varying points of view and differing perspectives. Lecturers draw attention to and interpret the important themes. Through examinations and assignments they influence which educational theories students learn about. Lecturers can select for teaching practice schools that correspond to their views of good practice. Students wishing to please the teachers with whom they are placed and their visiting lecturers, may well teach in ways that will earn positive reports, rather than in accordance with their own preferred teaching styles. What cannot be estimated is the extent to which students put on a 'show' when they know they are being monitored closely, only to adopt teaching styles totally unrelated to their initial teacher education courses once they become fully qualified.

Institutions for higher education do not relinquish their influence on teachers after initial training. They continue to provide post-experience courses, some of which lead to higher degrees. Generally though, it tends to be only a minority of teachers who have the time, inclination, and energy to attend these courses. Certainly to attempt courses of further study on a part-time basis at the end of a school day can be extremely draining, both physically and mentally. Furthermore, as Georgiades and Phillimore (1975) point out, a single, inspired teacher, fired with enthusiasm and determination after completing an in-service course, can quickly retreat, dispirited, into a shell, when faced with the cynicism and reluctance to change of colleagues. It is for this reason that Georgiades and Phillimore talk about 'the myth of the hero innovator'.

Readers may at this stage wish to reflect on the major influences on their own practice to date. Do initial teacher education courses influence how you teach? Did you embark on your course with views about teaching that changed in the light of your studies? Or did you tend to agree with those lecturers who offered perspectives similar to your own, and to discount opinions which challenged your own standpoint?

Institutions of higher education are certainly in a position to influence practice, but it is not clear how far-reaching their impact actually is. Students invariably have to spend many hours studying in their own time, so perhaps it is the literature they encounter that exerts a major impact on practice. Lecturers draw students' attention to a wide range of published material and research findings. Students are encouraged to read these when preparing for examinations, as part of their course work and in preparation for teaching practice, so let us now look at what gets published and researched.

What gets published?

Academic reputation depends on publishing. The low contact hours that lecturers have with their students, especially in universities, may seem to the outsider to be part of a privileged lifestyle. The purpose is, however, that staff may devote much of their energy to research and writing: a reflection of this is that so much of the educational literature on library shelves today comes from university lecturers.

Leaving aside for the moment the question of the extent to which the printed word actually shapes the development of the educational system, there is another question that deserves consideration, namely, what determines the content of books on education? As we have indicated already, there are themes that are nationally important. For example, there has been a growth in the number of books on teacher appraisal and the National Curriculum. Publishers will encourage, no doubt, those writers who offer something in these areas when they present an outline of their ideas. Possibly, some writers or academic departments that have shown interest or experience in these topics may be invited to submit outlines. There will be less commercial risk attached to such topics because they are pressing issues for teachers. As one moves away from such national interests, commercial viability becomes less certain.

It is through publishing books that might sell that the educational publisher not only stays solvent, but also exerts an influence over the information students encounter. However, we are not suggesting that the motives of the publishers are solely commercial. For some academic books, the process of publication amounts to a form of subsidy for material which might otherwise fail to see the light of day. Yet it is not too far-fetched to see that the economic climate for publishers will serve to focus their attention on what will sell. The books that appear in bookshops and in libraries are published within a system where new ideas have been judged to be marketable. Alexander (1984) comments on this and feels that in recent years publishers have played safe and have taken on only obviously marketable texts.

Apart from academic books about education, the publishing world produces teaching materials such as reading and maths schemes and, in general, textbooks and source books for use in schools. It is not clear what guides teachers in the selection of such material. Do they select books and materials that reflect their views of how to teach the curriculum, or does the available material dictate the curriculum? Perhaps it might be realistic to acknowledge that it is a combination of cost, what a teacher is used to, and what is immediately available, that dictates choice of material.

The influence that publishers have on writers, that books have on teachers and on the education system, and that the curriculum has on the education book market, is difficult to estimate. Lecturers, in recommending certain books, influence what their students read and this is part of the way that the higher education curriculum influences the school curriculum.

What gets researched?

University and polytechnic departments of education together with research, testing, and evaluation institutions, such as the National Foundation for Educational Research (NFER), vie with one another to secure research grants. It is to be expected that departments vary considerably in areas of interest, in different approaches to education, and possibly in promoting different educational values. We can speculate on whether this influences the selection of a particular institution, researcher, or department in an Institute of Higher Education, when research is commissioned. It might be the case that the DES, for example, decides that it requires a study to be undertaken by someone of no identifiable political persuasion. It might, therefore, commission research from an individual or department having no history of involvement in any political controversy. The commissioned researchers might emphasize their adherence to a view of science that is neutral, value-free, and takes them wherever lies the 'truth'.

Research that is funded is increasingly judged in cost-benefit terms. It would be naïve to expect that research is exempt from such accountability. There may be some projects for which the financial returns are not immediately obvious, but these projects are balanced in the portfolio by some 'nice little earners'. What are the benefits that accrue from educational research?

In university and polytechnic education departments, small-scale research may be undertaken by students completing higher degrees, sometimes contributing to some part of an area of study undertaken by academic staff. Such on-going interests will serve to provide the academic staff with a springboard for books and articles. This will help attract students to the department and might wave a flag to the DES and any other sources of research grants, that here is a department with some expertise. The skill is to choose relevant topics in which to become an 'expert'.

Central government and research

Governmental mind-reading helps researchers 'to be in the right place at the right time'. While this might contribute a (cynical?) explanation of why individuals and departments in education undertake research, it still does not answer the cost-benefit question as viewed by those commissioning research. What, for example, might educational research do for the DES? It hardly produces findings that have an immediate commercial application. One might understand why the government funds research into the storage of nuclear waste, but what does it obtain from research into educational provision for the under-fives or the use of computers with children with visual impairment?

Does the DES play the same role in respect of research as publishers play in respect of books – an altruistic concern to see knowledge flourish for its own sake? It might be cynical to argue that there is no interest in knowledge for its own sake, but it might also be naïve to argue that there are no other gains. Although there may be less commercial motives for commissioning research, the use of research findings to generate and support government policy is one possible reason.

To exert influence over what is researched, it is not necessary for the government to associate itself closely with those points of view that coincide with its own. It is sufficient for departments that produce 'acceptable' research to continue to be rewarded with funding. In fact, if there is any validity in the view that departments and individuals undertake research with one eye on what will attract funding, then it is likely that attempts to anticipate what is 'acceptable' will determine the nature of more research projects than those that actually receive the funds.

Through being a major source of research funding, the DES assumes a powerful position to influence the areas of research conducted, even if not the outcomes. Knowing what might attract funding maintains academic and teaching interest in those areas and, subsequently, publishers' interest. In this way, amongst others, the government can substantially influence educational ideas.

We have now looked at the framework in which education takes place and considered some of the ways educational organizations and institutions influence educational practice. We now look at the relationships and tensions existing between these elements in the light of the 1988 Education Reform Act.

Who controls the education system?

As we stated earlier, in the past education has often been viewed as a series of partnerships. Central government has worked in tandem with local government, which in turn has been in partnership with its schools. Parents have also become partners with schools in the education process. Although some of these partnerships have been strained at times, the fact that education has been a public service has implied that those employed in the public sector would harness their efforts with those of parents in an attempt to meet the needs of individual children.

At the moment, the balance of power has shifted away from local authorities towards central government and schools. The Secretary of State for Education and Science has assumed increased powers under the 1988 Education Reform Act. Similarly, schools also have greater autonomy and responsibility for a number of areas that previously rested with LEAs. In the future, the role of LEAs will entail checking that schools are functioning as they ought, in terms of both resource allocation and curriculum implementation. LEAs will be respondent to central government and to the schools themselves, rather than evolving and initiating policy to the extent they did in the past.

The transfer of responsibility from LEAs to schools for the administration of resources, while welcomed by some headteachers, may mean that schools will be faced with having to resolve conflict between political, administrative, and educational priorities. What makes good sense from an administrative point of view might not be good educational practice, and good educational practice might not be politically acceptable.

Central and local government have had long experience of juggling political, administrative, and educational priorities. More of the responsibility for this balancing act now falls on schools. In some ways, the responsibilities for pulling the education service in different directions, or, if you prefer a more positive interpretation, for keeping the education service in a state of dynamic tension, rested with clearly defined factions. In the LEA, for example, officers represented the need for organizational efficiency, politicians represented the political pressures, the Teacher Unions represented professional concerns, and so on. Under Local Management of Schools, some of these conflicts will be played out within the school itself.

The influence of the market-place

The shift in control of the education system brings a very different philosophy to bear on how education is to be conducted in the future. In the past, central and local government planned as best they could to provide a system of education that attempted to be egalitarian in nature. The aim was to provide equality of opportunity and government determined how best to allocate resources to achieve this.

LEAs had flexibility over how they funded the education service and could offer support to those schools that, for one reason or another, experienced difficulties in meeting children's needs. LEAs could therefore offer additional finances to purchase new equipment, improve staffing ratios, or put at the school's disposal various support services where a need was perceived. In principle at least, LEAs could assist all schools in making the best possible provision for the children under their care.

The concept of partnership and planning is now replaced with that of the 'market place'. Parents rather than children have become the consumers of the education services, and schools are now funded largely in terms of how many pupils they have on roll, with very little scope for LEAs to apportion additional resources to specific schools should it be necessary.

We now wish to look at some of the implications for those involved in education, given the shift in emphasis from education as a series of partnerships to a system whereby parents act as consumers.

Parents as consumers

The education system of the future is envisaged as a consumer-based service. Parents are now cast in the role of buyers who are 'purchasing' their preferred form of education. Just as it is assumed they will take their custom to the high-street shops that provide the best service, so they will now do the same in selecting schools for their children to attend. It is envisaged that parents will shop around and look for a 'best buy'. Parents also have power as a group to vote for their child's school to seek 'grant-maintained status' – to opt out of LEA control and to be funded directly by the DES.

Selling schools

The exercising of parental choice over where children are educated places schools in the position of having to become accountable for the service they provide. To take a business analogy, we can anticipate that schools in the future will attempt to offer guarantees of satisfaction, whilst at the same time employing promotional strategies to 'sell' the quality of their product. If parents are satisfied with the outcome of their children's learning, they will want their children to stay at the school. They will send their other children there and will recommend it to parents who may seek their advice.

Such accountability to parents is likely to increase competition between schools for pupils, particularly as the funding of schools is related directly to the number of pupils on roll. The 'good' schools are likely to flourish and those that are deemed 'less good' will have fewer pupils and so will struggle to survive and become less viable. Schools in many instances will be competing directly with other schools in their catchment area. Co-operation between neighbouring schools will give way to competition for clientele.

It may well be that the pamphlets schools are required to produce under the 1980 Education Act will change in nature. At the moment they are likely to contain details about the school's educational philosophy, patterns of organization, personnel, as well as basic information. In practice, they can vary from a few pages of cyclostyled print to a lavish brochure designed using the best of the school's desk-top publishing resources. In the future, state schools may follow the example set by those in the private sector and produce colourful, glossy brochures advertising their educational virtues.

It may also be the case that on the numerous occasions parents are invited to school activities (for example, educational festivals, parents' evenings, school performances in the arts, sports events), the emphasis will shift dramatically from participation and sharing a range of experiences to an occasion when the school's wares are carefully scrutinized and critically evaluated.

Perhaps the area of accountability likely to cause most concern for schools, particularly in the primary sector, will be the results of publicly reported assessments. Whereas these mainly affected secondary schools, except where selective examinations at eleven still applied, the establishment of assessment at seven, eleven, fourteen, and sixteen now includes both primary and secondary schools. It is likely that assessment results will be taken as the key factor in informing parents about a school's effectiveness. Securing 'good results' will be the barometer for success and failure and is likely to be the single most persuasive 'selling' indicator that parents will adopt.

Sources of consumer advice

The Education Reform Act has given schools more control of what they do but has brought with it a higher level of accountability. Giving parents increased rights and making schools accountable to them will only have the intended impact if parents feel in a position to exercise their new-found powers. The growing influence of parents is likely to be accompanied by an increase in potential sources of advice. There are already a number of centres that inform parents of their rights and guide them in their contact with both central and local government.

The Advisory Centre for Education (ACE) and the Campaign for the Advancement of State Education are both advisory organizations that provide information about a wide range of educational matters and submit evidence to official bodies, such as Committees of Enquiry. Summaries of important legislation by ACE, especially directed towards the consumer, have become valued documents for professionals too.

Not surprisingly, the Children's Legal Centre has also taken a lively interest in educational matters with a concern for the legal rights of children. This representation of consumer interests, both of children and parents, offers another means by which educational change is made accountable. Where these pressure groups strike a chord that can be amplified by the media, their views can exert considerable influence. This is one process by which politicians can sense the mood of their constituents, and convert influence into legislation.

Managing schools: The role of governors

The Secretary of State has been determined to ensure that the local community, especially the business community, shall have its views represented to the school through membership of the governing body. Governors have overall responsibility for employing staff (and dismissing them, should it be necessary); the 'conduct of the school' (Education Act, Section 16[1]), which can be seen as the range of factors contributing to the development of a school ethos; the implementation of the National Curriculum; discipline; parental complaints; and, in schools which qualify for financial delegation, control over the spending and accounting of the school's finances.

The position of governors is unenviable. They have considerable responsibility and power and yet are hardly experts on educational matters. They represent the non-specialist community involvement in education. Teachers are accountable to them and will need to recognize the criteria governors adopt in determining the successes and failures within a school. A lot will clearly depend on the headteacher being able to represent the professional viewpoint of staff.

Where does this leave teachers?

Our concern in this chapter has been to provide readers with our perceptions of some of the potential influences on the practice of teachers and the context in which they now have to work. In trying to spell out how aspects of the education system function and interrelate, we hope readers will be in a stronger position to clarify their own aims and consider their distinctive contribution to school life.

Our general message is that although many organizations and institutions have an interest in educational practice, teachers ultimately are the final arbiters of what happens in their own classroom. It is our view that despite all the changes, the main influence on a child's formal education is still the teacher in the classroom. Central government has provided a detailed framework in which teachers must operate, but the legislation has not been drafted in such a way as to restrict how teachers teach nor, we believe, the detail of what they teach.

The 1944 Education Act gave legal control of maintained schools to LEAs. The Education Reform Act is seen to take any vestiges of curriculum control out of the hands of the LEA. Commentators have differed in the extent to which they see control of the curriculum lying with central government or schools. Central government certainly has an increased say in curriculum content through the National Curriculum Council, although teachers have had some opportunity to comment during the consultative stages.

Nevertheless, despite this increase in central control, if the National Curriculum is seen as a framework into which a great deal more detail needs to be woven (which is our view), then teachers still have considerable autonomy to develop the curriculum content and to determine how to teach. The balance will be struck between this autonomy and the need to achieve success in terms of the Standard Assessment Tasks. It may be the latter, rather than the National Curriculum, which more effectively places a straitjacket on educational practice.

Chapter Three

Curriculum perspectives

In the previous chapter we looked at some of the elements of the education system and discussed the influence they exert on teachers. In this chapter we identify and examine three of the areas that those elements seek to influence formally in the classroom. These are

—— what is taught
—— how it is taught
—— assessing and evaluating what is taught and learned

We refer to the first area as the 'curriculum', the second as 'pedagogy', and the third as 'assessment and evaluation'. Although we will look at each area in turn, there are a number of themes which are common to all three. The advocates of a particular orientation towards the curriculum are also likely to favour certain approaches to curriculum planning, styles of teaching, and approaches to assessment and evaluation.

The philosophies which are reflected in the descriptions of the three areas have tended to be seen as polarized. Espousing one philosophy implies generally a criticism and rejection of another. We can also see how the language used to describe and discuss each area implies sets of values. These are issues we introduce here and explore in greater depth in later chapters.

Our desire to focus on the curriculum, pedagogy, and assessment and evaluation stems from our view that teachers have the opportunity to exert considerable influence over them. There are many other aspects of classroom life over which teachers can also exercise an element of autonomy, including the social dimensions of teaching considered in Part III. The curriculum, though, is an area that dominates the school day and is a major concern for everyone connected with education, particularly since the 1988 Education Act. Whilst this legislation has many implications for schools in the future, the National Curriculum is the one aspect of the Act that directly affects every teacher in the classroom.

Theories about what is taught, how it is taught, and assessment and evaluation, provide the background against which recent developments in education can be set. Our intention is to give readers an overview of the debate as it relates to these three areas, to consider them in the light of the National Curriculum, and to draw out the implications for classroom practice. In so doing, we consider what this might mean for the teacher who wishes to exert her autonomy and how she might avoid some of the inherent contradictions within the Education Reform Act, particularly as it relates to assessing and evaluating children's learning.

In Chapter Four we focus on psychological influences on the curriculum. Our discussion will highlight those aspects of psychology which have underpinned views on the curriculum, pedagogy, and evaluation and which have given rise to certain 'conventional wisdoms'. Our discussion will illustrate how debate is often conducted, and reflects one of the central themes of this book about the value of negotiating and resolving differing perspectives.

Views on the curriculum

Let us start by defining what we mean by the curriculum. The concept of the curriculum is wide ranging and can be seen to cover everything taught to children in school, whether intentional or not. The unintentional curriculum is usually referred to as the 'hidden curriculum' and represents values and beliefs that underpin much of what is taught, but which are rarely acknowledged openly. Of particular concern to those wishing to offer all children equal learning opportunities are the ways the 'hidden curriculum' can convey racist or sexist values. We will return to this issue later but now start by introducing four major perspectives on the curriculum.

The first view of the curriculum we discuss sees that there is a fixed body of knowledge which children should be taught. This knowledge represents 'truths' which are independent of individual learners and human experience. In a sense knowledge can be seen as 'God given', absolute, and principally unchanging. This concept of the curriculum derives largely from the writings of Hirst (1974) and Peters (1966).

Blyth (1984), in his overview of approaches to the curriculum, terms this view 'forms of understanding and endeavour'. He suggests that there are different ways of understanding knowledge which are independent of individual interests and experience, and also independent of each other. Included on any list of such forms would be empirical or scientific, mathematical, logical, literary, historical, aesthetic, moral, and religious understanding. This list overlaps with the subjects that have often formed a central part of the secondary school curriculum and are now embodied, to some extent, in the core and foundation subjects of the National Curriculum.

The view that there are established bodies of knowledge can be contrasted with another perspective on the curriculum which maintains that the learner, rather than forms of understanding, should be at the heart of any attempt to appreciate the nature of the curriculum. Knowledge, within this framework, cannot be prescribed with any certainty. On the contrary, it is acquired through experience and implies that it might very well be different for individual children. This particular approach to the curriculum has been advocated persuasively by Blenkin and Kelly (1987).

Within this perspective, knowledge is seen to be tentative and uncertain. Rather than being distinct from the learner, knowledge cannot be separated from the sense individuals derive from their experiences and discoveries. What is important is the process of learning, rather than what is learned. There are two strands to the learning process. First of all, Blenkin and Kelly (1987) propose that the curriculum should facilitate children's development, which encompasses personal, social, aesthetic and moral attributes. Second, it is envisaged that this will be accomplished through children's direct experience and discovery of their own world. This view of the curriculum has become known as 'the process approach'.

Alongside forms of understanding and endeavour and the process approaches to the curriculum, a third philosophy, referred to by Blyth as 'social imperatives', takes the view that what is taught in schools should reflect the needs of society as a whole. The curriculum is seen in instrumental, utilitarian terms and is very much driven by a desire to meet the requirements of society. The ends dictate the means and in its extreme form there is little room for reflection or deviation from the government-dictated orthodoxy. This view of the curriculum can, therefore, be seen as responding more to the needs of the community than to those of individual children.

In recent times in the United Kingdom, this has manifested itself in exhortations to schools to become more technologically orientated in order to prepare children for the world of tomorrow. Evidence for the emergence of this philosophy at the moment can be seen in the number of courses bringing the world of industry into the curriculum. Education and industry was a familiar partnership in the curricula of the 1980s and, one suspects, will be in the 1990s as well.

A fourth view of the curriculum is seen to offer the potential for initiating changes in society as a whole. This view has been adopted by those on the political right, as well as those on the left. Morrell (1989), for example, examines the distinctive ideological basis of the Education Reform Act 1988, and identifies social changes it is intended to promote, as well as learning opportunities it will deny to large numbers of children. Morrell, arguing from a left-wing perspective, sees that the

National Curriculum is designed to lend validity to a particular set of ideas, which fail to appreciate the reality of either the world we live in or the nature of our own multicultural society. She asserts that the National Curriculum, together with the framework advanced for assessing children's learning, will be socially divisive and give rise to an education system in which schools for different social groups are differentially funded.

In another context, Carrington and Troyna (1988) draw together a collection of papers which address what they term 'controversial issues'. These include considering the role of political education in the primary school, with particular reference to racism and sexism. The authors contributing to the book consider how these, and other issues, can be included in the curriculum and, in so doing, project a particular vision of society and the role of education within that society.

This brief picture portrays some of the thinking that has underpinned the way theorists have looked at the curriculum. Descriptions of the curriculum illustrate that the purposes of education are closely related to particular beliefs and values. The four approaches we introduce give prominence to the nature of knowledge, the learner, the needs of society, and promoting change in society. Each one gives priority to particular beliefs and values and the practical implication of these perspectives is not nearly so simple as adopting one to the exclusion of the others. In reality, there are competing demands made on teachers and children which are perhaps never resolved.

What we feel needs to be recognized is that there is no such thing as the value-free curriculum, that is, a curriculum which does not reflect a set of beliefs and values. Calls for the curriculum to be 'relevant', 'useful', or 'based on children's needs and interests', all imply certain values, depending on who is making the demands. A curriculum relevant to the needs of industry will be very different to one advocated by a social scientist. By whatever means the National Curriculum is interpreted and implemented in classrooms, teachers will be indicating what they feel is important and worthwhile, and consciously or unconsciously declaring their values.

We can see how this occurs, especially in relation to the impact of the 'hidden curriculum'. How a teacher takes account of gender, racial, cultural, and social factors, to make the curriculum accessible to all children, will be as important, if not more so, than his or her delivery of the formal content of the National Curriculum. One starting position, through which teachers can begin to recognize how they create equal educational opportunities, is by becoming aware of their own attitudes and values. However, what is clear is that, whether or not steps are taken to ensure equal opportunities, values underpin either course of action.

It is helpful to see the four perspectives on the curriculum as providing a series of templates with which to view the National Curriculum. The government has introduced the National Curriculum with definite assertions about why it is needed and what it will achieve (see Chapter Six on myths). The perceptions of individual teachers about what the National Curriculum will achieve are equally significant and dependent on a clear view of their own aims. It is, therefore, crucial that teachers clarify their intentions in the classroom.

Planning the curriculum

Prior to the 1988 Education Act and since the substantial reduction in selective examinations at the age of eleven, primary schools have had a certain amount of autonomy in determining curriculum content, despite the presence and influence of the elements of the education system identified in Chapter Two. In recent times however, teachers in secondary schools have probably had less choice due to the public examination system where syllabuses have given some indication of what is to be taught.

White (1982) has argued that, in a democratic society, curriculum decisions should not be left solely to teachers. It is a matter of common concern and as such should be opened up for public debate. Certainly there has been widespread agreement that there should be some form of common curriculum throughout the country for all children in the state sector to follow. The National Curriculum can be seen as a response to the call for common curricular experiences for all children, which had been discussed in a number of policy documents from the DES during the 1970s and 1980s.

It would be understandable if the impression created, from much of what has been said and written about the National Curriculum, is that all the decisions about what children will be taught have now been taken. We do not believe this to be the case. We see the National Curriculum for the core subjects of English, Mathematics, and Science as broad areas of study, rather than comprehensive statements of all that children should learn, as is often implied. The National Curriculum in the three core subjects includes statements of attainment, which incorporate the knowledge, skills, and understanding children should achieve. This demands that, in contemplating how to implement the National Curriculum, the promotion of children's knowledge, skills, and understanding must feature prominently in any planning that takes place. However, the statements of attainment are not comprehensive and so do not cover all the steps that many children need to learn as they progress through each attainment target. Teachers will, therefore, have to fill in the gaps, based on their understanding of how children learn and their knowledge of curriculum development.

In the past, when attention has focused on curriculum planning, two approaches have usually been presented. One approach is to set objectives for children's learning which concentrate on *what* they will learn. The other focuses on children's learning experiences and *how* they will learn. Within the objectives approach, a teacher's educational aims are translated into a series of tasks to be learned by the children. These tasks are often specified in behavioural terms and identify precisely what children will be able to do to demonstrate that learning has taken place. This gives rise to assessment procedures designed to determine whether those objectives have been taught to pupils and so leads to a form of accountability based on learning outcomes. This approach to planning is invariably associated with the types of curriculum described above as the social imperatives curriculum and, to a lesser extent, with forms of understanding and endeavour.

Advocates of a process approach to the curriculum have typically resisted specifying children's learning outcomes through the use of objectives. They argue that this cannot be determined in advance, as so much of what children learn will depend on their own responses to their learning environments. Furthermore, outcomes are secondary to the process of learning. Such a view, naturally, has implications for how children's learning can be evaluated and, thus, the forms of accountability that are appropriate.

Planning, within this philosophy, is geared to organizing the learning environment in such a way that it facilitates children's development. The teacher's knowledge is based on a sound appreciation of child development and the teacher has to judge each child's stage of development. The emphasis is on making learning meaningful, purposeful, and an active experience. It will be interesting to see how those who suppport this view will respond to the demands of the National Curriculum, since it specifies what children should learn at all stages of their education and requires formal testing so that their progress can be assessed.

The way these models are often debated conveys the impression that the objectives model is concerned exclusively with learning outcomes and the process model is concerned solely with how children learn and develop. These positions have often been presented as being mutually exclusive, with there being little in common between advocates of each perspective. What appears to be taking place in the light of the National Curriculum is a re-examination of these traditional stances because, irrespective of which models are favoured, objectives for children's learning are now enshrined in law. It is interesting that despite the emphasis on learning outcomes in the National Curriculum, the programmes of study published in connection with each subject emphasize the importance of the learning process. Children are required to apply their knowledge and to be actively engaged in their own learning.

It could be argued that the government, within the National Curriculum, has inadvertently acted as an arbiter between these two curriculum models, bringing together differing perspectives on curriculum planning. However, each model has distinct, and potentially conflicting, implications for deciding how to teach, and for assessment and evaluation, which we shall now examine.

Teaching methods (pedagogy)

Mirroring the views on curriculum content, two contrasting views have been expressed in relation to how children are to be taught. These views also embody strong statements of values and beliefs. One approach to teaching, related to the process approach to the curriculum, suggests that children need to be taught in entirely different ways since each child is unique and develops in a different way and at a different rate from others. For any given pupil, this would mean having individualized approaches to teaching, with methods being designed to meet the particular needs of that child.

Furthermore, it is argued that since each child is constructing his own understanding of the world, planning children's learning cannot take any form other than arranging appropriate learning experiences in which the child's own development can flourish. The classroom is then geared to stimulate children, to encourage interest, and to base learning on familiar everyday experiences. The teacher is a facilitator, promoting development and acting as the child's guide in the learning process. Investigative learning is at the heart of this approach to teaching. This concept of teaching has become known as child-centred (or learner-centred as described by Pope 1983) and has also been referred to as progressive. This philosophy was central to the views conveyed in the Plowden Report (CACE 1967).

The child-centred philosophy is usually contrasted with the teacher-directed orientation to teaching. However, within the spectrum of teacher-directed approaches there are two distinct positions which are ideologically very different. They encompass different values and beliefs but are frequently seen to be similar, because they are critical of aspects of child-centred education.

On the one hand, there are what are frequently termed traditional approaches to teaching, which aim to impart specific subject matter through methods which emphasize memory and rote learning, and where the pupils are largely passive. Education is seen to be about teachers disseminating skills, knowledge, and information which very much represent the beliefs, attitudes, and values of the dominant culture in society. It is the 'filling of empty vessels' concept. This approach represented the thinking behind the elementary schools of the past and remains central to a number of educators and commentators on education today. This traditional view of teaching has been welcomed by those on the political right and was advocated by the authors of the 'Black Papers' in the late 1960s and early 1970s in their challenge to the rise of progressivism.

On the other hand, this notion of teacher-directed education can be compared with the views advocated by Galton (1989), Simon (1985, 1986), and Engelmann and Carnine (1982). They argue, from their differing perspectives, for a change from what they see to be the relatively recent emphasis on the individual differences between pupils or teachers. Instead they advocate that general principles of instruction should be identified. Rather than looking at how children differ, efforts should be made to determine what it is that teachers do that leads to successful learning, so that principles of effective teaching can be articulated. In effect this would mean examining similarities which emerge in teachers' practices to see if these are underpinned by any generalizable principles. The emphasis, therefore, is less on differences and more on similarities. The concern is to develop a pedagogy which, for Simon (1985), is the science of teaching that embodies both curriculum and teaching methodology.

Simon, in his criticisms of individualized views of teaching, argued that it is impossible to develop general principles of teaching if each child is unique and so requires his own specifically designed teaching programme. Principles of teaching, Simon asserts, can only be developed through looking at what children have in common.

It is, therefore, important to note that criticisms of child-centred education stem from both the political left, such as Simon, and the political right, such as the authors of the Black Papers. Simon divorces himself from the authors of the Black Papers, whose views he describes as 'essentially philistine' and 'a-theoretical' (Simon 1985:97). However, he acknowledges that critics of progressivism are often identified with the Black Papers rather than the political left.

The development of a pedagogy is rarely advocated in HMI documents and the educational literature. In fact, there seems to have been a discernible reluctance to veer from the orthodoxy of emphasizing the importance of individual differences. It is a view that permeates much of current educational practice.

Although the child-centred philosophy of individual differences has been in the ascendancy, a number of studies (Bennett *et al.* 1984; DES 1978, 1982) have questioned whether its influence has been translated into effective educational practice. There would seem to be a number of question marks over whether the reality matches the rhetoric. Cohen and

Cohen (1986) in their edited book bring together a collection of articles that address this very issue. There seems to be a mismatch between what certain educators might want to happen and what teachers are actually able to deliver, given the day-to-day realities of classroom life.

Our discussion so far in this chapter has drawn attention to the fact that what we teach and how we teach are related to values and beliefs that we hold. If you are encountering these perspectives on the curriculum and pedagogy for the first time, you may already have formed some initial impressions about which philosophies you feel drawn towards. We would also like to remind you that, at this point, we are not attempting an analysis of the views presented. This will follow in the next chapter.

The implementation of the National Curriculum gives a sharp focus to the debate about curriculum and pedagogy. The question for many teachers is: how much freedom do I have over what I teach and how I teach? We have already mentioned in Chapter Two that, in our view, central government is not seeking to impose specific teaching method-ologies on the teaching profession. On the contrary, this is perceived to be the teachers' area of expertise: how they teach the knowledge, skills, and understanding, in the subjects comprising the National Curriculum, is to be determined by them.

One of our aims in this chapter is to illustrate that there is still much for teachers to decide and clarify, in accordance with their own values and beliefs, in implementing the National Curriculum. As we stated earlier, the concept of a 'National Curriculum' may be misleading, since it creates the expectation that much of what will be taught has already been established. However, in order to have legitimate influence over what they teach and how they teach, teachers will have to be alert to the impact of arguments that would seek to convince them otherwise.

 We now wish to look at how the issues surrounding assessment and evaluation may also exert a powerful influence on classroom practice. Past experience has shown that rigid forms of assessment, linked directly to teacher accountability, are likely to constrain teacher initiative and will ensure a narrow focus on the curriculum, with teachers adopting a highly directive style of teaching. Any tendencies towards this in the future may, however, be resisted by gaining an appreciation of the values which underpin different approaches to assessment and evaluation.

Assessment and evaluation

Before examining different stances taken towards assessment and evaluation, we need to distinguish between the two terms. Assessment usually refers to the process of gathering information on important dimensions of classroom life through a variety of means. Assessment might give us valuable information about a child's progress, or the effectiveness of our teaching, or a child's level of development.

Evaluation involves making judgements about what we have assessed. Assessment is often quantitative, evaluation qualitative. So we might assess a child's progress in reading and say what she has learned. We might then proceed to declare that the child's improvement is acceptable or that it is not what we might have predicted. When we make judgements and decisions about that child's progress we are moving from assessment to evaluation.

We also need to make a distinction between an assessment and evaluation of the curriculum and an assessment and evaluation of children's learning. The former may well incorporate the latter but this cannot always be taken for granted. As we shall see shortly, it will depend on the approach to evaluation adopted. Second, we need to recognize that an assessment and evaluation of either the curriculum or of children's learning, as well as being an integral part of teachers' work, can be undertaken by outside agencies during curriculum development projects.

We will first of all look at the models of curriculum assessment and evaluation carried out by outside agencies. This will highlight the issues that classroom teachers now have to address. We can place the various curriculum evaluation models under two broad categories which mirror the approaches to curriculum planning and adoption of teaching methods. The categories can be seen to differ in terms of their general principles and underlying philosophies.

The first broad category is the 'objectives model' which we introduced earlier in relation to planning the curriculum. The other side of the 'curriculum planning coin' is assessment and evaluation. Assessment determines whether set objectives have been learned by the pupils and the curriculum is evaluated in terms of whether it enables children to learn what we want them to learn.

Related to the objectives model is one which could be considered 'experimental', where different forms of educational provision are compared in a quasi-scientific manner. This requires some observable outcomes of teaching, which can be measured to help determine the effects of the differing types of educational provision under investigation. Whilst this procedure may be effective and desirable in the pure sciences, it is often much more difficult to implement successfully in relation to children and their learning. There are both ethical and practical considerations that can make such an approach difficult to apply in the classroom.

In contrast, the second category is illuminative evaluation. Here, evaluation tends to focus on a broader range of factors than children's learning outcomes and involves a range of techniques, including participant observation and the direct observations of evaluators. Evaluation addresses areas that would not readily lend themselves to the kinds of measurement required within the objectives model or an experimental, 'scientific' setting.

Illuminative evaluation is primarily concerned with description and interpretation (Parlett and Hamilton 1976). Researchers attempt to offer a detailed close-up view of life inside school and claim to focus on the educational process rather than the products of children's learning. Evaluation is not so much about what children learn, but the perceptions of people as to what is going on around them and the sense they make of education.

The models of assessment and evaluation which have been developed appear to have clear political overtones since they raise questions about the purpose of evaluation, who the information is for, and how it will be used. In this context it is helpful to consider MacDonald's (1976) views on evaluation and the ethical considerations that evaluators must acknowledge. He was concerned about how information was going to be used by those commissioning evaluations. He has argued that such evaluations cannot be value-free and need to be placed in their broader political context. MacDonald writes, 'I have increasingly come to view evaluation itself as a political activity'. He further states, 'Our task is to relate the style of an evaluation study to the political stance it implicitly adopts' (1976:126). MacDonald makes one other point that is pertinent to the themes we develop in this book, namely that there is a growing need for evaluators to make explicit their political orientation. In so doing they would provide a context in which their findings could be placed.

The models of evaluation introduced and MacDonald's views have usually been discussed in relation to large-scale curriculum development, evaluation, and research projects. They are of particular value to teachers now, given the demands being made on them and their developing role in formal assessment.

The extent of formal assessment undertaken by teachers has never been quite so widespread, or introduced so early in a child's school life, than is the case under the National Curriculum. Children's learning will henceforth be extensively assessed and reported, and it is likely that this measure will be a yardstick by which the quality of schools will be determined. Teachers, therefore, need to be mindful of the motives behind introducing the national assessments, who the information is for, and what purpose it will serve.

A regular aspect of a teacher's daily life is evaluating the outcomes of each school day on a number of criteria of significance to that teacher. Such evaluations tend to be informal and are not necessarily documented and available for inspection by others. This represents a private dimension of evaluation. However, today's educational climate requires that teachers communicate their perceptions of children's learning to a wide audience. The National Curriculum can be seen to herald the dawn of a new era in relation to assessment and evaluation. The 1988 Education Act requires that children's learning in the three core subjects of English, Mathematics, and Science be assessed through national tests to be administered at four key stages, when children are aged seven, eleven, fourteen, and sixteen. Children are expected to reach certain levels of attainment appropriate for their age. Nevertheless, it is stated that some children will fail to do so whereas others will progress beyond the expected levels. The results of the national assessments are set alongside teachers' own assessments of children's progress which will be moderated, so that the criteria adopted for assessing learning are standardized across schools.

A pressing concern for teachers relates to how children's progress is going to be monitored through the National Curriculum, in terms of both the national assessments at the four key stages, and the intervening years between national assessments, when public accountability will be less immediate. How children's learning is assessed is a keenly debated issue and focuses on the respective merits of two forms of assessment: normative (comparing children with each other) and criterion-referenced (finding out what children can or cannot do).

Much of what is currently known about assessment through the publication of the report of the Task Group on Assessment and Testing (TGAT) (DES 1988) has received a level of acceptance. This is largely because it endorses what may be regarded as good practice (Maclure 1988), with its emphasis on criterion-referenced and formative assessment rather than norm-referenced assessment. However, there is cause for concern, as we suspect there is an inconsistency between what is said in the report and what will actually happen in practice. Although the stated emphasis is on criterion-referenced assessment, it will be norm-referenced assessment at the four key stages that will form the basis of comparisons between schools. These measures have been introduced to provide a means by which one child's performance can be judged in relation to peers. Furthermore it is assumed that children's aggregated scores will serve as the indicator of a school's effectiveness.

Normative assessment, by its very nature, means that whatever the level of attainment identified for a given age, it is expected that some children will progress beyond that point, but also that some will fail to

39

reach that level and, thus, will be seen to have failed. This expectation is endorsed in the proposed system for assessment, which creates the expectation of 'failure' and builds this into the fabric of the education system. There is though, no reason to accept automatically the assumption of failure. While it is inevitable that some children will learn more than others, every pupil could nevertheless *be expected* to reach the attainment level for their age. There is therefore a real concern that, ultimately, the overriding emphasis will be on normative assessment at the four key stages because of how these results are to be used. For it to be otherwise would be akin to asking an athlete to forget about the Olympics every four years and concentrate on weekly club competitions instead.

This concern, that normative assessment will dominate, appears to be echoed when we look at the proposals for the teacher assessments. It is difficult to envisage how the teacher and national assessments will exist alongside each other. What happens when there is a lack of agreement between the two? Will the teacher assessments be set aside and give way to the national assessments? And if so, what will be the purpose of the teacher assessments if they can be discarded readily when they do not conform to the national assessments? In fact, if teacher assessments are moderated so that there is consistency between teachers and across schools, why have normative, national assessments? What purpose do they fulfil other than to undermine the validity and reliability of the teacher assessments?

It is not clear what form the national and teacher assessments might take at the present time. However, we share Morrell's (1989) feelings that the more appealing elements of assessment identified in the TGAT report will be sacrificed in reality and be seen as expensive, time consuming, and unworkable. Her concern is that this may then lead to a very narrow focus on particular outcomes which may in turn lead to sterile and unstimulating learning experiences for children, geared solely to achieving acceptable results on the national assessments. Whether or not this prediction comes to pass will depend to no small degree on the actions of teachers. This is the area we now consider.

The developing role of teachers

Teachers are becoming increasingly held to account by parents, governors, and LEAs for their educational practice. One way of meeting the challenges this presents is for teachers to appraise and evaluate their teaching extensively and demonstrate their involvement in a continuing process of enquiry, aimed at enhancing classroom teaching and ultimately children's learning experiences.

We have indicated in this chapter that there is still considerable scope for teachers to interpret and implement the National Curriculum in ways which do not undermine fundamental values. This would also apply to how teachers seek to evaluate their own teaching and children's learning. Teachers will increasingly be required to support their assertions about children's progress and perhaps provide details of how their opinions have been formulated. Parents are naturally distrustful of views about their children which are negative or different from their own, and uncorroborated in any way. In suggesting this we do not wish to be alarmist or to imply that such steps should be pursued for defensive reasons alone.

If teachers are to accept a wider evaluative role, they will need to extend beyond the boundaries and limits implied by the National Curriculum. We have indicated why we feel there is need for caution and even scepticism about the proposed assessment procedures, despite the attractive rhetoric of the TGAT report. If, as we suspect, teacher assessments assume secondary importance to the results of children's performance in the national assessments, teachers will need to draw on information culled from a wider source than is available from either normative or even criterion-referenced assessment.

Here we depart from the usual positive view of criterion-referenced assessment. Whilst criterion-referenced assessment is to be valued in so far as it informs what children have already learned and whether they are progressing, it does not perhaps provide a sufficiently detailed basis for determining *how they are learning*. Whilst we need to know what children have learned and how they are developing, teachers will perhaps also wish to know what learning experiences excite children, what motivates them, and what generally develops in children a desire to learn. In other words, teachers need to know more than simply what children have learned: they need to know the contexts in which children learn best and should be able to publicly account for their views.

If teachers wish to break from the traditions of normative assessment and provide a more complete view of children's progress, they need to look at each child's improvements, not solely in relation to peers, but with respect to that child's previous performance. Teachers may wish to concentrate their attention, and that of others, on how well children are progressing in relation to their own starting points.

We suspect that for assessment to be of maximum value it must do at least four things. First of all it must be part of everyday teaching and be readily incorporated into classroom life. Second, it must attempt to relate what children learn with how they learn best. Third, children must be partners both in the learning process and in assessing and evaluating their own progress. Finally, assessment must recognize achievement on a broader basis than is implied within the National Curriculum. Parents are generally concerned about their children's social and emotional development as well as their academic progress.

Such an approach to assessment and evaluation reflects our view that children should continue to receive a broad and balanced education which is not dominated by particular forms of assessment. However, if teachers are to broaden the scope of their assessment beyond that required by the National Curriculum, they will have to consider the extent to which their judgements will be accepted by others.

We have talked about assessment and evaluation as being the processes that provide information on which to base judgements about teaching and children's learning. Certain methods of assessment are probably seen to have greater credibility and power to influence and persuade than others. It is often felt that the use of normative assessment yields information which is 'objective'. Illuminative evaluation, in contrast, would be seen to be much more 'subjective', despite the steps which may be taken to meet such a criticism. Similarly, any teacher assessments which were unsupported by recognizably objective data would also be open to criticisms of subjectivity.

However, we must also recognize that the so-called objective measures can be queried on a number of grounds. The process of test construction helps to give them their credibility. However, we must endorse the views of Gipps (1984) and Levy and Goldstein (1984) who urge caution in the use of normative testing and warn against over-generalizing results. We would also advise readers to bear in mind the cautionary guidelines offered by Solity and Raybould (1988) in using tests, particularly in terms of relevance, administration, reliability and validity. Finally, it must be remembered that children react differently to being tested and their results do not always reflect what they are capable of.

In supporting this view, we are advocating that teachers collect detailed information on the teaching and learning processes in a manner not immediately implied by criterion-referenced assessment. We have discussed what we believe this entails and it shares some of the characteristics of assessment-through-teaching described by Solity and Raybould (1988). Teachers need to ask whether their opinions can be supported, whether they will be accepted by others, and whether what they are reporting is valid and reliable. In pursuing this path, teachers are beginning to adopt a 'research-based' role in the classroom. They are seeking to base their opinions on reliable and valid information which is related to their own teaching, to their assessments, and to discussions with, and observations of, children.

Our aim in this chapter has been to introduce some of the theoretical perspectives underpinning what is taught, how it is taught, and the assessment and evaluation of children's learning. What emerges are examples of what we term polarized thinking in relation to all three areas (i.e., product/process; teacher-centred/learner-centred; objectives-based/illuminative evaluation). We have further argued that teachers can still exert influence both in how they interpret the curriculum and in how they teach. To do so teachers will need to appreciate the influences brought to bear on them. With this in mind, we now examine the instances of polarized thinking we have identified and consider the influence of psychology on the teaching and learning processes.

Chapter Four

Psychology and the curriculum

In the previous chapter we looked at three areas: the curriculum, pedagogy, and assessment and evaluation. Our purpose was twofold. We wished to illustrate how values underpin practice in each area and that despite the imposition of the National Curriculum by central government, there is scope for teachers to evolve their practice in ways which accord with their own values. We suggested that there is still much that teachers can influence.

In this chapter we examine the way psychology has influenced debates on the curriculum, pedagogy, and assessment and evaluation. Our concern is with the way this debate is conducted, as well as the respective merits of particular ideologies. We will, in the main, illustrate the nature of this discourse, how certain views are advanced and others dismissed, by focusing on the impact in education of two psychologists, Piaget and Skinner, whose developmental and behavioural theories respectively, are frequently invoked in the curriculum literature. We will also look at the educational practice the theories have inspired, which will be discussed in the light of the National Curriculum.

We start by considering the influence of psychology on the curriculum and teaching and how the theories of Piaget and Skinner are introduced to teachers by curriculum commentators.

Psychology, teaching, and learning

Behavioural and developmental psychology have frequently been at the centre of educational debates concerning the nature of teaching and learning. The controversy has tended to obscure alternative interpretations and practical applications of Piaget and Skinner's theories and even possible areas of compatibility between them. As we indicated in Chapter Three, in the light of the National Curriculum, the potential for reconciliation needs to be explored.

Many writers have inspired various developments in process models of curriculum planning and child-centred education, but Piaget is the psychologist whose views have most influentially underpinned these educational philosophies. His theories of children's intellectual development have left an impressive legacy to the world of education, despite being subjected to rigorous, critical experimental examination, most notably by Donaldson (1978) and Hughes (1986). Piagetian influences in education are evident in the developmental, process, and child-centred approaches to the curriculum and teaching.

Behaviourism was first developed in the early part of the twentieth century by the psychologist John Watson. He felt that psychology should be concerned only with what could be seen and thus recorded directly. He advocated focusing on people's observable behaviour, rather than relying on reported mental experiences which had been the favoured methodology adopted by psychologists in their early attempts to understand human behaviour.

Behavioural psychology has given rise to the use of behavioural objectives in curriculum planning and assessment and is closely associated with teacher-directed education. The early work of Watson has been extensively developed by Skinner, whose theories about the nature of learning have had a major, albeit somewhat controversial, impact on the education system.

Describing psychology

In general, many authors whose work we have consulted imply rather narrow, less than favourable interpretations of behavioural psychology. They convey the feeling that they are more likely to have a good word to say about the 'Eurovision Song Contest', the Chancellor of the Exchequer on budget day, or the reliability of the British motor industry. Interpretations of behavioural psychology can be sharply contrasted with altogether more inspiring descriptions of child-centred education. We will now look briefly at a selection of what has been written about these two approaches.

Behavioural psychology

Barrow sees behaviourism as a 'rigid school of thought' and that 'behavioural objectives involve a narrow and mean-spirited approach to education' (Barrow 1984:134,138). He then goes on to say that:

a reduction of our planning to a systematic and detailed set of behavioural objectives is inherently trivialising and anti-educational; this is because the development of mind, the development of emotional and moral maturity, and the provision of a wide, but soundly chosen, set of experiences designed to encourage individual growth, with an emphasis on such qualities as critical spirit, self-direction, broad sympathies, insight and wisdom which are among the important aims of a school curriculum, cannot be adequately defined in behavioural terms, cannot be reliably recognised by behavioural signs and cannot well evolve in a setting that is predominantly bound by consideration of what can be immediately and readily observed.

(Barrow 1984:139)

Lawton sees the use of behavioural objectives as representing a 'conservative model, likely to appeal to those worried about standards, measurement and minimal competency' (1986:142). It is seen by Lawton to 'take the existing curriculum pattern more or less for granted, but aims to improve it by clarifying objectives, relating to specific changes in pupils' behaviour, and to evaluation' (ibid.).

Blenkin and Kelly write 'the first thing to be clear about is that the term "objectives" has come to be used quite specifically to denote short-term educational goals' (Blenkin and Kelly 1987:77). Then when talking about the objectives model of curriculum planning they comment, 'the focus of this approach to educational planning is on the modification of pupil behaviour' and 'a final feature of the behavioural approach to curriculum planning we must note is that like all scientific approaches to the study and planning of human activity, it endeavours to be value-neutral' (p. 79). Kelly, after stating what a developmental approach is, writes:

conversely therefore it [the developmental approach] does not see it as the central concern to engage in behaviour modification ... or to offer a diet of experiences justified only in instrumental terms, whether narrowly vocational or more broadly and subtly political, or to transmit subject/knowledge for its own sake.

(Kelly 1988:101)

Thus a picture of behavioural psychology emerges which suggests that: it is exclusively concerned with specifying short-term behavioural outcomes of children's learning; it is applied rigidly; it attempts to be value free; it narrows the curriculum; it is not concerned with developing essential personal qualities; and it is synonymous with behaviour modification and the use of behavioural objectives. How valid is this picture?

Early manifestations of behavioural psychology in the United Kingdom were in the form of programmed learning and behaviour modification. However, these were particular (and in retrospect, very limited and naïve) interpretations of the approach, which has now been developed and broadened. They are no more a part of current thinking amongst many behavioural psychologists than a MacDonald's beef-burger is an example of *nouvelle cuisine.*

It is certainly the case that many applications of behavioural psychology have been deserving of the criticisms they have received, although some of these criticisms have been founded on partial, limited, and historical information. We do not wish to challenge this or the veracity of what many of the above authors have written. Our concern is that they have invariably focused on a narrow interpretation of behavioural psychology and have selected certain examples as a means of discrediting the entire behavioural approach, rather than examining the varying justifications, perceptions, interpretations, and applications of behavioural psychology.

Descriptions of behavioural psychology such as Bull and Solity (1987), Cheeseman and Watts (1985), Child (1986), Engelmann and Carnine (1982), and Wheldall and Glynn (1988, 1989), represent a significant departure from the early simplistic explanations of learning, which focused almost exclusively on rewards and paid little attention to the context in which learning took place or the factors which facilitate learning. For these more recent writers, learning should be meaningful, stimulating, and flexible, and should encourage children to exercise choice and to become responsible for aspects of their own learning.

Developmental psychology and child-centred education

It is the child-centred approach which is seen to encourage children to make 'choices' and to 'take responsibility' for their own learning. Campbell describes what he sees as the basis for a child-centred approach to curriculum planning in the following terms; great value is placed:

> on the child's needs, interests and perceptions of the world in his or her own terms, all of which should be developed as far as possible unaffected by adult cultural forms. First-hand experience, individual differences, pupils choosing what to do, and discovery of knowledge by the pupils have the greatest priority.
>
> (Campbell 1985: 21)

Richards sees it as celebrating:

> self-expression, individual autonomy, first-hand experience, discovery learning, and personal growth. Compared to other perspectives, it advocates a much more equal partnership of teacher and taught with teachers, to some extent at least, learning 'alongside' children; it emphasises the processes of learning rather than

its products; and it offers children a relatively high degree of choice (though still somewhat circumscribed) in the type, content and duration of activities.

(Richards 1988:11)

For Kelly the developmental approach:

sees education as the process by which children learn to think, understand, to appreciate, to value and to do all those other things which most people would argue constitute what it means to be educated in the full and proper sense of that term.

(Kelly 1988:101)

To summarize, developmental psychology and child-centred education are seen to encourage pupil autonomy, choice, and first-hand experience, and the individual needs of pupils are given priority. We suspect that these terms convey a more positive and desirable impression than the ones which describe a behavioural approach. There is a language of child-centredness which implies total rights to certain linguistic terms and concepts. By inference, there is an implication that those who are not child-centred have not been concerned to encourage similar qualities in children.

Language exerts a powerful role in sustaining images of behavioural and developmental psychology. We now consider the impact of language a little further, together with other aspects of the debate surrounding these theories, that may well contribute to a teacher's appreciation and receptiveness to either approach. We start by examining the influence of what we have termed 'polarized thinking'.

Polarized thinking

What emerged during our discussion in Chapter Three was a sense that thinking is characterized by seeing educational issues as a series of either–or alternatives. Curriculum planning offers the choice between what children learn (the product) and how they learn (the process). Pedagogy presents us with teacher-directed and child-centred models and psychology provides behavioural and developmental perspectives.

We believe that the typical debate over these issues tends to reinforce existing prejudices. The dialogue is conducted in the manner of a political dispute. The language of political invective is adopted by those in educational circles to discount the claims of one theory and assert those of another. Although the subject matter is different, the language and manner of political discourse is often emulated. Rarely are possible routes to reconciliation examined. We see this as unfortunate because an appreciation of both theories can, in our view, make a significant contribution to educational practice.

Golby (1988) in his article about traditions in primary education, considers how educational theory tends to deal in 'over simple categories of an either–or nature', a point we echo in Chapter Six on myths. Golby quotes Darling who suggests that one oppositional stance, the progressive-traditional classification, is seductively simple. Darling writes:

> To begin with it legitimises a confrontational style of educational debate in which abuse of the other side is common, and the re-examination and refinement of one's own views is not. The opposition is rarely given credit for having a case which is even prima facie respectable, either intellectually or morally, and this is coupled with a refusal to admit even minor difficulties or weaknesses in one's own position.
>
> (Darling 1978)

Darling continues that more energy goes into attacking the opposition than reflecting on one's own stance. We can substitute the progressive–traditional distinction with any of the examples of polarized thinking we have presented and the points discussed by Darling would still be pertinent.

Polarizing views tends to pre-empt any attempt to examine either the dynamic tensions which characterize confrontational stances or to explore the possibility that one approach might be more appropriate than another on some occasions. Furthermore, and perhaps more importantly, it may mask any analysis of values and beliefs which may be shared, but which are rarely acknowledged during emotive verbal exchanges. We feel that the values related to different views have yet to be fully acknowledged and considered, due to the manner in which the debate has taken place.

Not only is our thinking often polarized, it can sometimes be of the 'nothing but' variety. We will illustrate this by focusing briefly on the work of Kelly (1988 – not to be confused with George Kelly whose work we discuss in Chapter Nine) who writes passionately about the process model of curriculum development. We do so not only because of Kelly's commitment to his position, but also because how he writes illustrates something of the 'nothing but' philosophy, which pre-empts any possibility of discussion or negotiation about his perspective.

Let us start by looking at the way Kelly writes about the developmental approach:

> it sees all knowledge as transient, as shifting, as evolutionary and thus argues for an approach to education which not only recog-

nises these characteristics of knowledge but also acknowledges the need for education to take full account of them and to facilitate the continuous development of knowledge which this view entails. Thus knowledge becomes almost synonymous with understanding and is something developed by each child (and indeed adult too) rather than acquired by him/her in some ossified form.

(Kelly 1988:101–2)

This can be contrasted with what Kelly then goes on to say about different approaches to education or those who have interpreted the developmental approach in a different way to him:

the incompatibilities which we have just noted are absolutely basic and central, so that compromise solutions are not possible; they are oil and water or chalk and cheese. If the differences go as deep as the fundamental views adopted of knowledge, of human development and of education, then any attempt to conflate them must lead to illogicality and incoherence of both theory and practice ... thus, too, all those suggestions, that we can plan our curriculum by the use of 'process objectives' (Barnes 1982; Skilbeck 1984) reflect a failure to understand how deeply the ideological differences go, or at the very least a use of the term 'process' that no developmentalist would accept.

(Kelly 1988:113)

Kelly articulates a clear stance in relation to developmentalism. However, any approaches to developmentalism which differ from his reflect a failure to appreciate the extent of ideological differences. Knowledge is transient, but seemingly not the theories of Piaget. It is likely that our interpretation of developmentalism which follows will be seen by Kelly, not as reflecting our continuing understanding of developmentalism, but rather our failure to understand altogether. There is little scope for fruitful discussion and negotiation when views are expressed in such a form.

So far the behavioural or developmental, teacher-directed or child-centred classifications have been discussed in relation to mainstream education. However, a different picture of these distinctions is conveyed through considering their impact on the field of special education.

Two contrasting views are usually advanced to account for the difficulties children experience in school. The child-centred, developmental, individualistic perspective on teaching and learning supports the view that there is something wrong with the child which prevents learning taking place. This position follows from an emphasis on individual differences between children, particularly where the nature of their differences is rooted in their intellectual development. Difficulties are viewed as the result of children not having the ability to learn. This has given credibility to the intelligence testing movement and the concern with normative assessment in general.

The second view asserts that the cause(s) of failure can be located in some features of the child's learning environment, rather than the child. Aspects of the curriculum may not be appropriate or the teaching methods selected may not be suitable. This explanation is the one closely associated with behavioural psychology. Applications of behavioural psychology in the classroom have demonstrated that many children who were initially thought to be experiencing difficulties make excellent progress when aspects of the learning environment are adapted to meet their needs.

Those who advocate adopting behavioural principles to teach children regarded as having difficulties, and those who are concerned to develop a pedagogy (particularly Engelmann and Carnine 1982), adopt, in our view, a more desirable position in relation to children and their difficulties. They start from the belief that all children can learn, and that they only fail to do so when the teaching they receive is in some way inappropriate.

The role of developmental and behavioural psychology in special education, underlines the fact that an examination of the contributions of either theory to educational practice has to consider the underlying motivation of teachers in adopting one approach rather than the other. It is not only a matter of observing existing practice but also of asking what is to be achieved by children and ascertaining the implications for those children, if we fail to realize our goals.

Psychology and the curriculum

In the discussion that follows, we may appear somewhat defensive of the behavioural perspective and more critical of a developmental, child-centred one. This impression, if it is conveyed, stems from a desire to reflect the wider applications of behavioural psychology whilst, at the same time, pointing out some of the problems associated with a developmental perspective. This arises because we are faced with one model that is generally favoured and another which is not. The balance of the discussion might have been reversed had opinion been weighted differently.

We wish to examine some implications of behavioural and developmental psychology in relation to the curriculum. We also consider the ways fundamental concerns are acknowledged and addressed within a behavioural framework and refer to the values which can underly practice from a behavioural perspective. We start by discussing a question which has to be confronted by any theory claiming to account for how children learn, namely: how do we know learning is taking place? In so doing we examine a fundamental tenet of behavioural psychology – focusing on the observable.

How do we know children are learning?

Behavioural psychology focuses on what can be observed as a means of determining whether children are learning. Their behaviour indicates to us the characteristics and qualities they have acquired and learned. There are limits though to this assertion, and these we now consider. Barrow, a critic of behavioural psychology, writes:

> It is quite true that for much human activity behaviour is the only criterion that we have whereby to judge what is going on. Am I walking? Watch me. Am I jealous? What can you do but watch my behaviour? But it does not follow, and it is not true, that all matters can be fully or adequately characterised in terms of behaviour.
>
> (Barrow 1984:135)

We now look at some of the limitations in focusing on what is observable.

Problems which arise when focusing on what can be observed

There are a number of difficulties in relying solely on behavioural indicators when seeking to determine whether the personal qualities and attributes we wish to encourage are being developed. One problem is in identifying, in any quantifiable way, the subtle forms of behaviour that indicate that a child is learning, for example, to be expressive, autonomous, or co-operative. Then there is the additional concern of reaching agreement with others that the behaviour we have identified actually measures what we wish to measure and is, therefore, valid.

Similarly, we have difficulties in how we measure. We only have 'snap shots' of behaviour rather than a continuous 'video'. We cannot easily follow children around and observe their behaviour under different circumstances, so our picture of the child is inevitably incomplete. As a result, even if we agree on behaviour that is consistent with certain qualities, we cannot observe it all the time to see if it is displayed appropriately and consistently. This can be further complicated when a child behaves differently with us than with other people. The behaviour we then see will be different and so may lead us to draw different conclusions about the child's development.

Furthermore, when we observe others, even though we focus on their behaviour, we may 'see' things differently. We do so because we interpret our observations as we try to make sense of them. We cannot readily separate what we see from our interpretations of what we have seen. Two people may interpret the same behaviour quite differently, or different behaviour in the same way. How any one of us makes sense of our personal world is an extremely complex process depending on many factors, some of which we may not be aware of (we discuss this in detail in Part III).

It is difficult to gain access to these personal processes and the way they have developed. The behavioural position, therefore, focuses on what can be seen, although this provides only part of the picture. The way we can give greater validity to our judgements about children's learning is by observing them over time and under various circumstances.

Are people's feelings and emotions ignored through focusing on what is observable?

Teachers are concerned for children's social and emotional well-being, as well as their academic achievements. How, though, do we judge what people are feeling or their emotional state? When you observe a child's behaviour, it is difficult for anyone to know what you might be thinking or feeling. Furthermore, and this is perhaps crucial to an understanding of the behavioural perspective, even if you try to describe thoughts and feelings there are problems.

Skinner drew attention to this during an interview with Dr Anthony Clare in the Radio 4 programme *In the Psychiatrist's Chair*. Skinner was in a bar having a drink with his brother. Within fifteen minutes his brother was dead from a brain haemorrhage. During the interview Skinner talked about the difficulty he had in describing his feelings at that time. He suggested that whether anyone would have any inkling about how he felt would depend on a number of factors. It would depend on how well he was able to identify his feelings and the adequacy with which he could describe them verbally. However, whether the listener heard them as Skinner intended would, in turn, be determined by the listener's understanding of language. The words used by Skinner to describe how he felt might correspond to very different emotions in somebody else. Can we assume that the language people use to describe their feelings conveys an accurate account of that individual's emotional state?

Barrow states that 'it is not true, that all matters can be fully or adequately characterised in terms of behaviour' (Barrow 1984). We can acknowledge this but are then left wondering whether there are alternative ways of assessing emotional states other than through observing behaviour? Similarly, is there any way of assessing learning other than through focusing on children's behaviour? These issues we now consider.

Learning and behavioural objectives

Behavioural objectives identify what children need to do to demonstrate learning has taken place. Their role is to help clarify intended learning outcomes and reduce ambiguity and confusion. It is thought to be helpful for both teachers and pupils to have some indication of where their endeavours will lead. Many educationalists have been reluctant to use behavioural objectives for the reasons we have indicated. However, what other means is available to ascertain learning has taken place without referencing this to some aspect of a child's behaviour?

The National Curriculum for each subject contains statements of attainment. Many of these are expressed in terms of what children should know, solve, compare, express, and use. A number of other verbs convey the knowledge, skill, and understanding children are expected to acquire. How will teachers know whether these attainment targets have been reached? It is likely that they will have to consider a range of activities and tasks that children might be expected to complete in order to satisfy themselves that the children are learning.

In developing tasks which indicate that children are learning, teachers will be confronted with a similar challenge to the one faced by Hughes (1986). He provides a fascinating account of his investigations into children's understanding of mathematical concepts. At one point he quotes Skemp in support of a line of enquiry he pursues: 'The criterion for having a concept is not that of being able to say its name, but that of behaving in a way indicative of classifying new data according to the similarities which go to form this concept' (Skemp 1971:27, Hughes 1986:41).

Now this seems to be an observable, behavioural way of establishing whether or not children have acquired a particular concept, namely to focus on their behaviour in a range of settings and see if it is consistent with the behaviour we expect from someone who has learned that concept. The interesting point here is that in reading this quote you may naturally think Hughes quotes Skemp to support a behavioural perspective. However, from an earlier passage in Hughes' book there is every reason to believe that he is not sympathetic to behavioural psychology. He writes about Thorndike's (whom he describes as a behaviourist) account of how children learn arithmetic: 'as with other aspects of behaviourist theory, practice followed by reward is considered the most likely mechanism by which the bonding would take place' (Hughes 1986:18).

The way Hughes draws our attention to dated, behavioural

psychology, with the emphasis on rewards as facilitating the learning process, is in line with the other descriptions of behavioural psychology which we have already discussed in this chapter and which do not readily acknowledge its broader perspective. What is of interest to us is that throughout the book Hughes articulates the behaviour he expects from children who have learned the various mathematical concepts in which he is interested, together with the contexts in which they might be displayed.

Whilst is it undoubtedly the case that a number of examples of objectives-based teaching have been less than inspiring, it is difficult to escape the fact that learning is verified by observing behaviour. What needs to be recognized are the limitations of this. Before leaving our discussion on how we ascertain whether children have learned, we would like to say a brief word about whether learning outcomes have to be pre-specified.

Do learning outcomes have to be pre-specified?

Many applications of behavioural psychology to children's learning in the United Kingdom have been in the area of special education. In this context there has been a particular rationale for specifying learning outcomes in advance, and in behavioural terms. Quite clearly, though, much of what children learn is not pre-specified, and teachers should be urged to encourage and welcome outcomes other than those they have already pre-determined. Equally, the quality of classroom life would be much poorer if teachers were unwilling to depart from planned lessons when the need arises.

However, the National Curriculum has put this issue in a different perspective. The broad framework for what children are to be taught has been incorporated into the National Curriculum. The attainment targets pre-empt debate about specifying objectives. Again, it is to be hoped that previous experience on this issue is not ignored and that the attainment targets are not followed slavishly, so that teachers feel unable to respond to children's interests and curiosity in ways which might require departing from pre-planned objectives.

We now wish to turn to a concept that is central to the child-centred philosophy – the focus on the learning process – and examine the tensions which exist between developmental and behavioural perspectives. This is a complex area and we would strongly urge readers who wish to pursue our discussion to consult Pope's (1983) paper on the objectives model of curriculum planning and evaluation. He discusses these themes in relation to developing a conceptual basis for educational technology and develops the issues we introduce here.

Are there intended outcomes of the learning process?

A major assertion within developmental, child-centred education is that it is concerned with the processes by which children learn rather than the intended 'outcomes' or 'products' of their learning. It would be difficult to maintain however, that there are no intended 'products' of child-centred learning. They may not be the same as those derived from a behavioural approach, but a teacher is working towards certain 'outcomes of learning'.

There are at least three ways of looking at intended learning outcomes. One is to focus on *personal qualities that children acquire*. These might include a desire to develop self-expression, individual autonomy, or a concern for others. Thus the anticipated outcomes or products of children's experiences in school would be that they displayed self-expression, autonomy, and a concern for others. This view of learning outcomes would be shared with the two that follow.

Another way of looking at outcomes is for teachers to concentrate on *developing specific processes that promote cognitive development*. The starting point in this case would be a thorough knowledge and understanding of children's intellectual development. It is developmental stages that become the teacher's goals and are the products of children's learning and educational experiences. So a teacher would be concerned that the children demonstrate that they can conserve, engage in formal operations, and think abstractly.

A third view of outcomes from the learning process requires that *teachers work towards set objectives which reflect children's knowledge, skills, and understanding*, as is done in the National Curriculum. For example, if children are taught science, it would be of less importance what scientific facts a seven- or eleven-year-old might learn, than that they were engaged in a process of enquiry and began to articulate *how* they might begin to investigate problems that are posed. However, this view also recognizes that children will only achieve outcomes of this type if they have acquired certain skills and knowledge, particularly in the area of language and mathematics. In this way, outcomes reflect that the child is learning general principles which are then generalized and applied in different settings. Our interpretation of a behavioural perspective would embrace this view of learning outcomes.

In all three views intended outcomes can be achieved through a learning process characterized by the use of discovery methods, first-hand experience, negotiation between teacher and pupil, and the teacher guiding the learner through purposeful, meaningful experiences. So we could walk into a classroom, observe, and note that all the learning activities were process-orientated. Although teachers' intentions and certain details of the activities would be different (to account for the different intended outcomes), learning would be facilitated through exactly the same process in all three instances.

For Blenkin and Kelly (1987) the main justification of any learning experience is that it promotes a child's intellectual development. Experiences which focus on curriculum objectives are only acceptable in so far as they help teachers achieve the goal of facilitating development. However, those focusing on curriculum outcomes would be concerned to ensure that children learn how to learn, through acquiring knowledge, skills, and understanding. They would not address hypothesized mental stages of intellectual development.

We suggest that describing any single approach to teaching as being exclusively concerned with either the process or objectives (which we have also termed intended learning outcomes) is misleading. Both developmental and behavioural approaches have clear ideas about what children are expected to learn. Similarly, to say that the one is child-centred and the other teacher-directed is also inaccurate. Curriculum outcomes can be attained by recognized child-centred approaches. Equally, the realization of developmental outcomes is achieved through a teacher's careful planning of children's learning outcomes. Whilst it cannot be assumed that children will learn or develop in the manner intended, extensive planning takes place to facilitate the learning process.

The nature of the debate on developmental and behavioural psychology implies that developmental psychology is child-centred and concerned with the learning process. By contrast, behavioural psychology is only interested in what children learn. Maintaining this position fails to recognize some of the limitations of a developmental perspective or the potential strengths of behavioural psychology.

We now summarize the view of the behavioural psychology that has been presented so far. A behavioural perspective can be seen as offering a starting point that helps teachers, parents, and children clarify fundamental concerns. It highlights the difficulties in determining and describing what and how children learn, the difficulties associated with describing feelings, and the fact that our knowledge of children is invariably incomplete and related to our own perceptions of life. Thus, describing a child as confident, self-assured, aggressive, or intuitive, can be seen as a shorthand for the behaviour we have observed but also reveals something of ourselves and how we have interpreted the actions of children.

The criticisms levelled at behavioural psychology, the issues it fails to address, are, we believe, pertinent to other perspectives as well. They have perhaps been expressed most forcefully, and even virulently, about behavioural psychology because its aims are more readily specified in a precise way. The rhetoric of behavioural psychology has certainly been less appealing than that of other theories of how children learn, and perhaps this has in some ways made it a ready target.

The values underlying a behavioural approach depend not so much on features of the theory, as on the values of those wishing to adopt its principles in the classroom. It can be interpreted narrowly and restrictively, as can any theory (including a developmental one). It can be construed in very different terms. Those who perceive that it is controlling, concerned with punishment and about modifying behaviour, have a different set of values to those who see that it could encourage a positive framework, in which punishment has no role whatsoever, where teacher, parents, and children work together in fostering children's personal, social, and academic development, so that they become autonomous, expressive, confident, responsible individuals.

One possible reason for the widespread adoption of behavioural psychology in the field of special education was the sense of optimism and purpose it was seen to embody. It recognizes that children who are thought to experience difficulties in learning can learn.

Behavioural psychology provides a framework for assessing whether children are progressing academically and socially. It is suggested that by making explicit and open to inspection what children are to learn and the processes through which they are to learn, teachers will be helped in facilitating and realizing their goals.

Developmental psychology and education: a cautionary note

We now briefly highlight some of our reservations about a child-centred, developmental approach. These concern whether a developmental view imposes limits on what children are capable of learning, how successfully individual needs can be met, and the apparent difficulties associated with the classroom implementation of a developmental, child-centred philosophy.

Learning-readiness

Egan (1983) offers a cogent criticism of Piaget's influence on education. He looks at key Piagetian concepts related to children's development, to their cognitive structures, to the role of active learning, and to the concept of learning-readiness. He argues that many of the claims made by Piagetians and developmental educationalists are untenable and cannot be sustained when subjected to critical analysis. He sees the frequently offered interpretations of development as restricting and imposing limitations on children's learning, rather than being in any way facilitative of it.

It is argued that notions of learning-readiness sanction the non-intervention of teachers. Instead of acting to facilitate and stimulate learning, teachers are recommended to wait and to allow children to develop at their own pace. Direct involvement is withheld and only encouraged when children demonstrate they have reached the appropriate developmental stage.

Simon (1985) draws attention to this point. He suggests that the view of learning-readiness embodied in the child-centred philosophy represents a convergence in thinking with the theories embodied in the intelligence testing movement. Both, he argues, are based on the premise of learning-potential which determines the rate and level of learning. Potential is seen to be fixed and the intelligence test is the 'scientific instrument' which indicates this potential. The concepts of learning-readiness and learning-potential, create expectations about what children might typically achieve and imply that teacher intervention will not significantly alter the course of children's learning and subsequent levels of achievement.

Meeting individual needs

When we look at the demands of providing appropriate learning experiences for every child in a class, we have to question how realistic this may be. Harlen when talking about the match between learning experiences and levels of understanding defines matching as:

> finding out what children can already do and what ideas they have, as a basis for providing experiences which will develop these skills and concepts. The keynote of matching is thus finding the right challenge for a child, the size of the step that he can take by using but also extending existing ideas. There is as much a mismatch if this step is too small, leading to boredom, as there is if it is too large, leading to failure.

(Harlen 1982:184)

Will this be possible in every curriculum area for every child in the class? The indication is that it is proving extremely difficult to achieve from a developmental, child-centred perspective.

The study by Bennett *et al.* (1984) is particularly in this respect. They observed sixteen teachers, all of whom were judged to be better than average by local authority advisers. The teachers of six- and seven-year-olds were keen advocates of individualizing learning and yet an appropriate match between children's attainments and the demands of tasks in language and number work was only evident in approximately 40 per cent of the tasks given.

Matching was worse in the first term of junior schooling (children aged seven to eight), where the proportion of matched tasks in number work fell to 30 per cent. The incidence of mismatching was particularly marked for those children seen to be high attainers, since three-quarters of the tasks they received underestimated their existing level of achievement. Teachers were invariably successful in recognizing that a task was too hard but were said to be 'totally blind to tasks whose demands were too easy' (p. 215). Teachers assumed that if children were busy, the work was at an appropriate level.

In conclusion, Bennett and his colleagues pointed out that the philosophy of children 'working at their own rate' meant that many low-attaining pupils experienced a less varied curriculum than more academically advanced peers. This meant that they were being denied educational opportunities which were available to other pupils.

Rhetoric and reality

The rhetoric of child-centred education is undoubtedly appealing and yet it still has to be translated into widespread educational practice. Various HMI surveys (for example, DES 1978) and research projects (Barker-Lunn 1984) have questioned the extent to which practice reflects the rhetoric, and although there may be criticisms of their research methodologies, we are left to ask why there appears to be such a large gap between what people say they are going to do and what they actually do.

Galton (1989) also examines the extent to which progressive education was adopted within primary education following the publication of the Plowden Report in 1967. He considers a number of different explanations that have been offered to explain the 'reality-rhetoric' gap and cites one which is based on the views of Simon. He calls this the 'lack of theory theory' and suggests that the lack of a pedagogy prevented teachers from effectively pursuing the Plowden philosophy.

We are suggesting, like Simon and Galton, that if difficulties in implementing child-centred approaches are to be overcome, the theoretical basis underpinning practice must acknowledge the limitations of focusing on individual differences between children and their 'learning potential'. Instead it must emphasize the benefits of deriving general principles of teaching, which can help all children experience success at school. A question raised in this chapter, is whether our interpretation of a behavioural approach has any part to play in this process.

In this chapter we have illustrated how developmental and behavioural psychology are introduced to teachers and we have discussed their respective contributions to theories about teaching and learning. We have suggested that accounts of behavioural psychology are often based on partial, narrow, and dated interpretations of the approach, which effectively undermine any exploration of the distinctive contributions either psychological perspective can offer. Through failing to acknowledge the specific areas developmental and behavioural psychology address, or the values that underlie applications of either approach, teachers are necessarily less well equipped to resist exhortations to adopt principles from one theory, to the exclusion of the other.

In this book we are concerned to make explicit some of the processes that influence how teachers make sense of educational practice There are questions that have to be answered as a part of teaching, irrespective of theoretical stances adopted towards the curriculum. Our purpose in drawing attention to an alternative interpretation of behavioural psychology has been to suggest there is value in exploring the examples of polarized thinking we identified at the beginning of the chapter, with a view to examining areas of compatibility rather than differences. Of equal importance is our wish to draw attention to the values which underlie our interpretation of the approach. We hope that a consideration of these values will help to redress the balance in future debates about the status of behavioural psychology within education. We believe teachers are potentially empowered through embracing a broader interpretation of behavioural psychology, recognizing how it complements other perspectives, and acknowledging its role in enabling the extensive demands of the National Curriculum to be met.

Part II

In this section, Chapters Five, Six, and Seven look at teachers and teaching from the perspective of how practice often has a basis or rationale that is unclear to the practitioner. Chapter Five explores the way values underpin educational practice by examining how evidence, supporting the way things are done in education, often bases its validity on scientific procedures. The chapter argues that science itself cannot be value-free. The way in which business organizations reveal or hide their values is also looked at and an argument is made for the benefits to both business and education of establishing an ethos that is clear and public.

In Chapter Six, we look more closely at how current practices are based on history and on functions that serve a social psychological purpose. These functions help organizations to establish an identity, to resist change, and to maintain cohesion. Finally in this section, we consider how language also reflects values. We examine its potential for clarifying or obscuring meaning and its power, as an analytical tool, for identifying influence.

Chapter Five

Values

In previous chapters we looked at some of the structural features of the education system as sources of influence on schools and on the classroom practice of the individual teacher. We also looked at how theories, particularly in relation to the curriculum, are made to appear exclusive and to confront other theories, by their supporters. Important as an examination of the structure is as a starting point, we have suggested that practice is not only determined by structure, by connections, by physical components, but also by social psychology.

In their study 'Fifteen Thousand Hours', Rutter *et al.* (1979) argued for the concept of an *ethos* as a way of explaining an essential quality in schools. In their view, the concept of ethos is a way of thinking about schools as social organizations (pp. 183–4). Rutter and his co-authors recognize, as we do, that a structural description reflects, but is insufficient to capture, the spirit of the educational system, the school, the classroom, or the teacher.

This chapter is concerned with values, with the way that we all go to such lengths to keep from each other some of the important influences on the decisions that we make. Some of the personal influences on the individual's decision making are described more fully in Part III. In this chapter we explore some of the ways that, in our view, decisions are made in the public sphere of education and become transmitted to the area of the classroom. Many of the areas of debate in education are discussed not so much at the level of fundamental values, but as matters of evidence. Protagonists present arguments and evidence as if they were involved in a dialogue determined by the rules of science. Since this scientific mode of presenting evidence characterizes how much of the discussion proceeds about educational issues, we feel that some examination of those rules is necessary, hence the section on value judgments and value-free science.

We begin by looking at what we mean by values. We then turn to the issues surrounding positivism and relativism regarding scientific evidence, terms that we shall explain in that section. From there, we go on to look at values in organizations and in systems, reflecting the view that understanding of the educational system may be gained from looking at the broader context of other organizations and systems. We then turn more specifically to values in educational practice and relate these to the classroom, where, according, to *our* values, all educational theory is put to the test.

Defining values

Max Weber, the German sociologist, advocated that, in the social sciences, value judgements should play no part in the presentation of objective data. In this context, value judgements may be described as statements or decisions that reflect an element of the social scientist's own views on the subject matter that she is studying. The value is an expression of worth about the matter in hand. For example, if we undertook a study of the association between intellectual performance and environmental lead levels, and we happened to use the term 'lead pollution', it might be seen as revealing something of our values about lead's undesirability, at a time when we were specifically investigating whether or not it had an undesirable effect.

Values are judgements that we make about the personal worth of events that we experience. Our framework for evaluating the world may be enormously complex as we make distinctions of worth between Shakespeare's sonnets, between different types of spaghetti, between two screwdrivers, or between carpets. It is to be hoped that our conceptual framework is sufficiently rich to provide us with many different dimensions on which to make our judgements of worth.

As will become clearer from later chapters, the basis on which we make our value judgements may not be totally at a surface level. Where our values come from may not be obvious, even (or particularly) to ourselves. These judgements reflect our emotional reactions to aspects of the world and influence both our attitudes and our beliefs. While the distinctions between attitudes, beliefs, theories, and values are not easily made, we see them as follows.

Beliefs and theories represent our attempts to provide ourselves with accounts of the world. They help us make sense of life and provide us with a basis for predicting future events. Whereas our theories are possibly less emotive, more rational, and more capable of being tested than our beliefs, both are underpinned by our values. Both are evident in our attitudes, which can be seen as consciously held responses to aspects of our experience and which we can put into words and discuss. For example, you may have an attitude towards rock music that it is an immature form of musical expression. You may believe that it undermines the moral integrity of the young. Your theory about rock music is that the rhythms and the loudness cause neurological changes that cause people to become disinhibited. Your values, which are to do with the innocence of youth, the need for high moral standards, and the need to protect young people from their own excesses, obviously contribute to your theories about the world, your beliefs, and your attitudes.

It will suffice for our purposes if we define values as those aspects of life, tangible and intangible, real and imaginary, that we see as being worthwhile, that we might wish to work for or otherwise promote. Much of our interaction with the world is based on, or produces, responses from us which have an evaluative dimension that might be as straight-forward as liking or disliking, or might be much more complicated. Whatever the foundation for the judgement, it can be reduced to a dimension of good or bad. For the most part, we do not need to put into words or even think about evaluating every aspect of our existence.

Try this exercise. Stop reading for a moment and look around at some of the objects near to you. How many of them cannot be judged in terms of some of their qualities as good or bad? For example, this desk has a reasonably good sheen on it, but badly needs to be dusted. The lamp gives a good light, but is badly adjusted.

Now that your attention has returned to this text away from your surroundings, we hope we have caused you to focus on some of your, at least superficial, values. It is possible that some of the items that you have been looking at are very dear to you and are highly valued by you for all sorts of reasons. If that is the case, begin to think what makes those items so personally valuable. In thinking about this question, you may have found yourself being drawn down into some of your deeper and more central values. The point is that we hold values at many levels, but the central, more fundamental values prop up more of our beliefs, attitudes, and theories about the world than do our superficial values.

Value judgements and value-free science

Scientists are accorded credibility and an independence of view. Through science, our culture has fashioned for its own use a tool which is perceived as being objective and value-free. Our culture assumes that the scientific method is a sufficient safeguard against the unwarranted intrusion of personal values and beliefs. Scientists declare the basis on which their hypotheses have been formed, the nature of the hypotheses, the methods of data collection, the results and the conclusions that they have drawn. This procedure is accepted as a short-cut through endless discussion on the validity of the evidence and, hence, furnishes that evidence with protection from enquiry into the values that might influence it.

In a later chapter, we shall be looking at the work of George Kelly as a way of coming to an understanding of how values influence the views of the individual. Kelly is critical of the positivist view of science, the view that evidence is evidence and that there is an objective basis to our experience. In an essay he wrote:

> So the business of the scientist is to get things nailed down, one at a time, and, using each established fact or law as a point of departure, to make further inferences and test them by experimentation. If the data confirm the hypotheses, then one will have something more to nail down, and the total job of simulating the universe will be that much nearer completion. I suppose when the task is complete they hope to declare a scientists' 'sabbath' and rest from their labours.
>
> (Kelly 1977:10)

Kelly uses the term 'cumulative fragmentalism' to describe this process of nailing down pieces of knowledge. Sir Karl Popper, whose philosophy of science is very influential, is also opposed to the idea that knowledge becomes nailed down. He takes the view that what we know, in the sense of our theories about the world, are simply the best that we have at this time and may be supplanted by better theories as more evidence comes to light. In his view we should be looking for evidence that *disconfirms* our theories.

We raise these issues about science because so much of the debate about the major issues in education revolves around the question of evidence rather than around the question of values. There appears to be an acceptance within the educational world of the positivist viewpoint that evidence is evidence, that there is a bedrock of data that can be used as the source of arbitration.

One strand of our thesis in this book is that evidence is negotiable. To that extent, we support the relativist position – a view that the knowledge that we have of the world is not universally true and enduring for all time, but is valid only for us and only at this time. We recognize, of course, that there are aspects of our common experience for which it is useful to act as if we share the same perceptions. Some of the confusion in interpersonal communication arises, none the less, when we make assumptions about how other people see things, without checking out these assumptions.

We see people as struggling to make sense of their world and in so doing they are aided by enormous powers of interpretation. It is in our view unlikely that we can set aside these powers of interpretation, or train ourselves to use them in such a totally constrained way as the positivists or Weber would wish us to do. Once we accept the position that, for each of us, our experience is unique, that our ways of viewing evidence cause us to make individual interpretations, it leaves us another philosophical problem: how do we ever agree about data?

John Heritage (1984) draws our attention to the solution proposed by Schutz, the sociologist. Schutz argues that people interacting with others may make two basic assumptions that help them to act as if they live with the same experiences of the world. The first is that if they change places they will have the same experiences and they will see the world in the same way. The second assumption is that any differences that might exist arising from unique biographical experience can be viewed as irrelevant and can be set aside for the purposes of that interaction.

Clearly, these assumptions provide a means of making progress in the negotiation of knowledge. We may have different life histories and different values but there are ways of progressing towards agreement on the basis of assumptions about the commonality of experience.

So far, we have argued that much of the discussion in education draws on matters of evidence and is conducted as one might conduct debate in the sciences. We have declared our values, and indicated that knowledge and evidence cannot be assumed to be value-free. Moreover, we have stressed the importance of negotiation regarding evidence, recognizing that events in the world can be seen from different angles by different people and can be interpreted differently. There may be ways in which groups of people share common experiences that others have not had. There may be ways in which individuals are unique. There are times when the commonality of experience is to be celebrated and times when individual uniqueness is to be recognized. None the less, for understanding to occur between people, assumptions about how others see things have to be checked out and not taken for granted.

Earlier in this chapter we also mentioned the term 'ethos' as signifying that not only individuals but also organizations can hold and promote values. We turn now to look at organizations, but before focusing on schools, which are of course our main interest, we look at some of the parallels in commerce and industry. We turn to examples from business partly because there are accessible examples to draw on, and partly because we feel that the use of analogy can help to throw light on our main topic.

Values in organizations and systems

Education is an industry. In this country, it is the largest source of local authority employment, to which total may be added the numbers employed by universities, the independent school sector, and central government. It occupies substantial plant, consumes vast financial resources, and manages the whole of the nation's progeny from five to sixteen. Learning and day care are its twin services. It is in regard to these two elements that its output or quality of service can be judged and to that extent it is no different from any other large organization. If one views education as a large industrial conglomerate, then some of the ways of analysing the operation of organizations may shed light on education.

What, then, are the features of industry, of business, or of other large organizations that might have relevance to education in terms of values? First, there is the sense of corporate identity. This is the ethos of the organization. It is what draws people to join that organization; it sets the standards of the business; it helps customers or consumers to identify the organization and its goods and services and to identify with the organization. A catalogue from a manufacturer of high-quality furniture will stress the marrying of traditional skills with the evolution of more modern approaches and equipment. The emphasis will be on care, and the company carefully constructs for itself a metaphor of the craftsman. A Japanese manufacturer of electronics and electrical goods, including televisions, hi-fi, and microwave ovens, will emphasize the robotics of its manufacturing process. The corporate identity, here, is one of being right in the forefront of technological progress with precision at all cost.

Another method for the organization to project its corporate identity is through the process of recruitment. Adverts will say much about the values of the organization. The picture that may be painted of the qualities of the successful applicant may have little to do with the day-to-day demands of the job itself, but will reflect the ethos of the organization. Some of the adverts seek to involve potential applicants in a process of thinking themselves into the role. Thus there may be reference to a scenario that will involve the eventual post-holder, indicating how that person will be expected to solve tricky logistical problems, be prepared to work long unsocial hours, go beyond the call of duty, and display qualities that will deter the average human being. Here, the overall impression is that you need to be superhuman to work for the company.

There is a further feature of the organization that relates to values, namely the process of instilling loyalty. J.A.C. Brown (1954), writing about the social psychology of industry, draws attention to the strong feelings of corporate loyalty, both towards senior managers and towards the products of the firm by its employees. Similar views have been expressed by employees when they have secured orders against strong competition. The winning of an order reinforces a sense of pride in a company. One of the criticisms that Brown makes of British management is the failure to harness this loyalty to the firm, but where it is employed, it can be a powerful mechanism for reinforcing the values of the organization.

In their influential study of top business organizations in the United States, Thomas Peters and Robert Waterman (1982) also emphasize the importance to management of deciding what the company stands for. Organizations develop values or are constructed with a value system. Successful organizations make their values clear, and, however chaotic their structure, according to Peters and Waterman, they maintain a tight coherent set of core values within the organization. A major aspect of any organizational analysis is to look at the shared values of that enterprise.

It will be interesting to see how long it takes for education to catch up with business. Schools, through the legislation giving them increased financial delegation and management, have the opportunity to take on a more business-orientated approach. Education authorities, also, may find themselves competing within a market framework to provide services to schools. As educationalists come to terms with having to operate as business managers, will they learn any of the lessons from industry? Peters argues that one difference between a major US retailing organization and its much more successful rival was that it had several levels of management, whereas the more profitable company had just a three-tier structure.

Will we see a reduction in all the different allowances and grades that exist in schools and education departments? The other point we have made is about the importance of deciding company values and conveying them clearly to staff and customers alike. Perhaps, as schools vie for pupils following open enrolment, we shall see more effort on their part to indicate to parents just what the school stands for. One aspect highlighted by the studies into successful companies is the value that these companies place on their staff. Surprisingly, successful business is looking increasingly conscious of people. It would be nice to imagine that our educational institutions might also progress in that direction.

Having made the case for the importance of values in business, let us look more closely at how this translates to the world of education.

Values in education

One major problem that besets the educational system and differentiates it from the business world is the nature of its political control. For success, organizations need to be managed within a stable and coherent value framework. For success, no violent tugging at the steering wheel is required, just a gentle nudge here and there.

David Hargreaves, Professor of Education at Cambridge University, has made a case for regional management of education, taking it away from the control of local authorities, with their ideological about-turns at every local election. His is not the first voice to be raised against the excessive intervention of politics in education. And yet education is a political issue. Unlike the manufacture of steel, the production of coal, or the running of trains, the very process of education is political. To educate the nation's youth requires decisions to be made about the content of the curriculum and the methods of teaching.

Attempts are made, and continue to be made, to disguise the values that are enmeshed in education. Prior to the Education Reform Act of 1988, there was, for example, considerable effort on the part of the government to play down the political aspect of the Education Reform Bill prior to its enactment. In an article in *The Times Educational Supplement* examining the constitutional significance of the government's legislative proposals, Jackson Hall, former Director of Education for Sunderland, wrote:

> Mr Baker's argument appears to be that there is no need for concern about the constitutional issues because the Bill's objectives are educational. For example, he referred to the national curriculum, declared that 'its purpose is educational', and asserted that 'it is not concerned with the distribution of power'. Does he not see that the prescription of a national curriculum (whatever its merits) in legislation is a decisive shift of power? Why does he think that the churches campaigned for religious education to be a foundation subject?
>
> (*The Times Educational Supplement*, 1 April 1988)

What Jackson Hall is doing so effectively is acting as a customs officer and challenging Mr Baker, who has elected to present himself in the 'green channel' as having nothing to declare. Hall is demanding that Baker should 'come clean' about his real intentions, his real values concerning the legislation that he was introducing. In fact, it is probably fair to point out that the Conservative government had not concealed their values in broad terms, and Baker's mistake was to depart from the government line of relating every component of their legislation to their basic values. Perhaps, on that occasion, Baker genuinely felt that there were no political issues to do with the introduction of a National Curriculum! If so, this underlines our view that attempts to bury the values on which educational decisions are made have become habitual.

It is doubtful whether much security or stability will be gained by altering the political accountability of education from local authorities to regional control, as Hargreaves suggests, or to central control, even though the Thatcher government has gone some way towards the latter with the Education Reform Act. The very purpose of education is inseparable from politics. Education confers power. Access to higher education provides a substantial probability of higher earnings. Education shapes the thinking and attitudes of young people at a highly impressionable age. Teachers wield power to direct the future political development of people and hence the political climate of the nation. It is argued that amongst other factors the success of the Labour Party at the 1945 election stemmed from the politicization of the troops prior to demobilization through the process of education. It is for these reasons that careful control is exercised over what is taught, how it is taught, and to whom. Education has the potential to change governments.

There are other instruments of public opinion, of course, apart from education. Newspapers and television also exercise political control, and are free to do so. Education is not free to exercise political influence, partly perhaps because its charges are considered to be naïve and vulnerable. It is possible, however, for proper political education in schools, even at primary level, to begin to educate children in the skills of identifying manipulation, propaganda, hidden values, and faulty argument. Why is no education available in these fundamental skills which, some would argue, are the keystone in the democratic arch? Is it that to provide children with the tools of political analysis would make them less susceptible to propaganda (and to advertising)? Would it lessen the impact of the media on public opinion and hence shift the balance of power?

As long as there remains no vital, dynamic programme of innoculation of our young from undue political influence, there will remain the problem of how to control the curriculum. The perceived removal of the curriculum largely from the local authorities towards central government only serves to heighten anxieties, since at a stroke, the government has the means to control what is taught nationally. It requires confidence that the checks and balances at Whitehall are better or as good as those at County Hall. We have argued in Chapter Three, of course, that the teaching profession, itself, *does* act as a balance to central government control in relation to the curriculum.

The issues concerning the influence of values in education are broader, however, than simply curriculum control. For example, the organization of education into either comprehensive or selective schools is an issue underpinned by values, as is the question of testing and assessment. Yet another issue that exemplifies the influence of values concerns the fundamental purposes of education. This was illustrated in our discussions in earlier chapters on the nature of the curriculum. A further expression of fundamental values is embedded in the question of whether education does actually influence society – of whether one can use schools as a form of social engineering. An examination of some of these issues will serve to illustrate the involvement of values within education.

Comprehensive schooling

Debates about comprehensive education have continued for at least the

last fifty years or more under one guise or another. Part of the issue
hinges on the value or otherwise of selection at eleven. Brian Simon
recounts the controversy surrounding the discovery that Sir Cyril Burt
had 'fudged' some of his data. Simon points out the influence that Burt
had on both the Consultative Committee of the Board of Education and
on the Spens Report on Secondary Education (1938). Regarding the
influence on the Consultative Committee, Simon states:

> it is necessary to recall that Cyril Burt was the leading psycho-
> logist whose evidence as to the nature of children's intellectual
> capacities was preferred to and consistently accepted by the
> Consultative Committee to the Board of Education in the inter-
> war period. This 'evidence' was reflected more or less precisely in
> important recommendations by the Committee in favour of
> developing a divided system of secondary education and, in
> particular, of imposing rigid forms of streaming in primary
> schools. It provided, in fact, the theoretical rationale for the
> selective and hierarchical system of public education as it was
> developed at that time.

In respect of Burt's influence on the Spens Report, Simon writes:

> Equally important, the crucial Spens Report on Secondary
> Education (1938), which proposed the tripartite system,
> specifically acknowledges a similar memorandum by Burt on the
> age-group 11–16 (p. xvi). This, says the Committee, 'forms the
> basis' of the chapter in which the Committee proposes the
> separation of children over 11 into different types of secondary
> school. Thus it was Burt's psychometric evidence that provided
> the rationale for this proposal.
>
> (Simon 1978)

Burt's evidence had sufficient influence on the shape of public
education in this country for the exposure of its unsatisfactory nature to
have major repercussions. Simon paraphrases the views of Alan and
Ann Clarke, expressed in *The Sunday Times*:

> ideological convictions as to the power of heredity were held by
> Burt with such striking power as to blind him to the elementary
> requirements of scientific procedures both in the collection and in
> the presentation of evidence. In this sense the revelations as to
> Burt's procedures and practice bring into the clear light of day the
> full extent to which ideology has penetrated into this field of
> science – even of its dominance by strongly held presuppositions
> of enormous social and political significance. The liberal view

that science is unaffected by, or neutral in relation to, ideology has received a very severe blow indeed.

(*The Sunday Times*, 24 October 1976)

We make no apologies for raising again the issues surrounding the Burt affair, and, as psychologists, we have a particular interest in the way that psychology has served education. There are a number of lessons to be learned from the misuse of scientific prestige, perhaps particularly at the moment when some political and educational analysts would see, behind government thinking, an eagerness to turn back the clock to the old tripartite model of education, through the establishment of City Technology Colleges. There is a suspicion that despite the well-publicized intention that these schools should reflect the spread of abilities, in fact they will move, through their processes of admission, towards a more selective intake.

If the evidence behind the tripartite system stems from an authority whose values were clearly in favour of segregated education and yet who presented evidence as if totally neutral to the issues involved, it serves to underline the need to exercise the greatest care in accepting evidence where there is no declaration of values. Simon, in subtitling his book *A Marxist Critique*, leaves no one in doubt as to the origin of his analysis.

More recently, the debate about comprehensive versus selective education has re-surfaced with claims by Baroness Caroline Cox and Dr John Marks that civil servants at the DES organized a campaign to discredit the evidence that Cox and Marks had presented in 1983. Their evidence, based on 1981 examination results from a sample of fifty-seven local education authorities, indicated that pupils matched in terms of social background, attending secondary modern and grammar schools, obtained 30–40 per cent more O-level passes than those at comprehensive schools. It is alleged that the DES prepared a confidential report on the research, and criticized the sampling and the social class weightings used by the authors. Cox and Marks were not given a copy of the DES report, even though it was given to the press and quoted in Parliament. The authors subsequently received 'profuse private apologies from the DES' (Celia Weston, *The Guardian*, 27 December 1988). Baroness Cox and Dr Marks have published a pamphlet through the National Council for Educational Standards in which they warn that this case is an example of 'the insolence of office in contemporary England'.

It is possible that for Cox and Marks their target is not only to set the record straight on their work, but to illustrate how devious public servants are. This might be part of a consistent campaign by the government and its supporters to undermine confidence in the concept of neutrality of officers at the DES. After all, there have been a number of instances of civil servants in other departments not toeing the line. However, such speculation is not the central purpose for our inclusion of this example. Yet again the debate is conducted around the validity of the evidence. Both sides are playing the game according to positivist rules. If you can demonstrate some inadequacy in the scientific nature of the data, you can discredit your opponent's case. Our argument is that the evidence will be already contaminated by the values of those that are submitting the evidence. It is not possible to eradicate the bias, therefore authors should declare their bias.

To summarize the argument so far, education is big business. It is political both in terms of, on the one hand, the power involved in managing such a large slice of the nation's economy and, on the other, the very nature of the educative process itself. The established view seems to be that, since education has the power to propagandize, it needs to be controlled. Efforts are made to keep politics out of education, in terms of the way issues are presented to pupils. There is no doubt that party-political issues must be handled with care but how do teachers deal with issues that strike at the very heart of their values? Some means of presenting both sides, as happens for packs about nuclear energy, may need to be developed for other political topics. However, politics within the curriculum are in danger of being sanitized – presented in a way that removes them from everyday events. Just as sex is taught as being part of a relationship, perhaps politics should be taught as being a part of everyday life.

Clearly, education itself remains a political issue. The response within education is to suppress any declaration of values. The game is played like a game of radio-controlled boats on a park pond. All the discussion is at the surface level, while underneath the water, powerful nuclear submarines manoeuvre round each other looking for an opportunity to strike. Evidence on which decisions are based – to organize education this way or that, to develop this aspect of the curriculum or that, to teach according to this method or that – is evidence that necessarily has been influenced by values. These values need to be declared as part of the process of submitting evidence.

Values in the classroom

Let us turn briefly to look at values as they impinge on the classroom. The teacher is subjected to influence from many sources. She is responsible to the headteacher and to the governors of the school. The headteacher may, to some extent perhaps, delegate power to teachers in terms of how they will interpret the school's curriculum in the light of LEA guidelines and now of course, the National Curriculum. Teachers, solely or through their departments, will be answerable to local advisers and sometimes to HMI for the quality of their work. Each will feel a direct responsibility for the progress of her students and will feel answerable to parents as well as to the students themselves. She will feel influenced most of all perhaps by what she has learned from her own education and her training as a teacher, by what she gleans from the trade press, from books about education, from her colleagues in the school, and from courses and lectures that she attends from time to time. All of these sources of influence reach her rarely as first-hand direct experience. They are parcels of knowledge, little packets of information that have derived from other people, from people who have a different view of the world, different experiences, and different ways of selecting information from all that they perceive.

What does the teacher do with all this information, for there is no doubt that much of it is redundant, much of it contradictory, much of it difficult to make sense of? She sifts it and selects that part which is meaningful to her. We shall look at some of the influences on her personal selection later in the book. The point here is that she selects according to her values. She may, of course, play the education game, in which case she will tell herself, and everyone else, that her practice is based on such-and-such a study which showed such-and-such a result. She will believe that the evidence that she has been given by all the education experts was free from political, moral, ethical, and personal considerations. If she plays the education game according to the rules, she will not question the fundamental issues that are contained in questions about daily practice, but believe that practice stems from evidence and that the evidence as far as it goes was produced in good faith by someone seeking to conform to Weber's notion of value-free, objective social science. On the other hand, she might begin to ask questions about where the evidence and the ideas are coming from. She might begin to ask questions about the values that she holds in terms of what she has selected to incorporate into her own practice.

The next chapter goes on to look in more detail at some of the practices in the classroom and in schools. It seeks to demonstrate that practice is governed by more than straightforward rationality. What this chapter has attempted is to make the case that, even when practice is based on rational decisions from objective evidence, powerful influences are operating in terms of fundamental values. These values are not bad and do not need to be eradicated. After all, the evidence from what Peters and Waterman (1982) regard as excellent organizations is that these corporate values should be made clear. And this is our message too. The educational system and educational organizations need to declare their values as do those individuals working within them.

Chapter Six

Myths, rituals, and routines in education

The previous chapter looked at the importance of values as determinants of organizational practice, both in relation to education and, more broadly, in relation to business. The theme underlying that chapter and this current one is that the behaviour of the individual teacher in the classroom is subjected to considerable indirect, implicit and, sometimes, covert influence. Unlike later chapters, where the source of some of that influence will be identified as relating to the individual herself, we shall continue to look at aspects of the organization that may be exercising influence. This present chapter pursues this theme by looking at some of the practices that exist within education and seeks to encourage the reader to ask questions about them: about why they came into existence; why they have been maintained; and what explanations are currently offered for them.

Paraphrasing the words of George Kelly, it is not behaviour that is rational, so much as the explanations for that behaviour. We shall put the case that much of educational practice has very little formal theoretical or empirical foundation. It has grown out of tradition rather than from carefully observed study. It is, of course, consistent with our theme that we do not criticize practice simply because it arises out of individual or collective values, rather than from some 'scientific' basis. We expect practice to reflect values, whatever the rational basis for the practice. What we do seek to challenge is reasoning after the event, which attributes a theoretical or empirical basis to practice, so as to obscure the values that actually determine what goes on.

For the teacher in the classroom, time is precious and opportunity too infrequent to be able to seek out the academic origins of ideas influencing education. The teacher may be tempted to take much for granted, to focus on the practical rather than the theoretical. In this way the stage is ideally set for the teacher to be subjected to influence, to be overawed by history and status, rather than be empowered by critical appraisal. As a contribution to helping teachers look at what goes on in education with detachment and in terms of how practice relates to their own values, we turn our attention to myths, rituals, and routines.

A word about myths

First of all, a word of explanation is needed to clarify the terms we use. The most difficult term is that of 'myth'. The word has come to be understood as applying to a story or account of the world that has grown up without needing proper evidence. Its use in this way is not unlike the use of the term 'conventional wisdom'. In everyday language, myths have a grain of truth in them, or in some way appeal to those who tell them and those who hear them, but, like a snowball on the top of a mountain, have rolled into a much greater story than their origins justify. We do not necessarily quarrel with this use of the term, but we also add to it a particular meaning that derives from the work of social anthropologists.

For social anthropologists, such as Malinowski, the term 'myth' has a technical meaning and this is how we should like to use it. This technical usage of the term 'myth' refers to the process whereby stories or accounts of the world grow up within a culture. In terms of how we wish to use the term, it does not matter how far these myths have their basis in fact.

By now, the reader will be aware that we see fact and truth as relative, depending on one's personal perspective and experience. Myths may start from some real event or grow from other sources: it does not matter which. What is important about myths is not that they are wrong or out of all proportion to their origin, but that they are active and become a mechanism of control within the culture. Membership of a group is determined by subscribing to the myths of the group. Having the right to recount the myths of the group is a powerful indicator of the acceptance of the individual within the group. Myths help the group to achieve an identity, a common set of values. To this extent, they are the 'stories' that belong to the group. We do not see myths as true or not true. We do not see them as good or evil. They exist as a means of regulating society, of determining who is and who is not a member of the group, subgroup, tribe, culture, subculture, clique, or tennis club.

Writers have documented some of the myths that are to be found in education, and, in particular, we make reference to a book by Arthur Combs (1979), entitled *Myths in Education*. Combs identifies a number of myths, but subtitles his book *Beliefs that Hinder Progress and their Alternatives*. His view of myths is that they get in the way. Our view is that they may do or they may not, but that is not the point. The point is that they will not go away. They are a necessary part of society. Like

Combs, we feel that it is important to identify myths. However, if by identifying myths we wish to eradicate them altogether, that, in our view, is a mistake. Whatever account one uses to replace a myth is yet another myth, another view of the world, the belief in which shapes the membership of the group to whom that myth belongs.

Max Gluckman quotes Malinowski's views on myth:

> Myth fulfils in primitive culture an indispensable function: it expresses, enhances and codifies belief; it safeguards and enforces morality; it vouches for the efficiency of ritual and contains practical rules for the guidance of man. Myth is thus a vital ingredient of human civilization; it is not an idle tale, but a hard-worked active force; it is not an intellectual explanation or an artistic imagery, but a pragmatic charter of primitive faith and moral wisdom.... The myth (as against folk-tale and legend) comes into play when rite, ceremony, or a social or moral rule demands justification, warrant of antiquity, reality, and sanctity.
>
> (Gluckman 1965:283)

The way in which we use the term takes it out of the context of so-called primitive culture and into our own. We see myth as a mechanism for justification in the way that Malinowski does. Malinowski implicitly compares the process of myth within primitive culture with the 'scientific' or 'objective' process of accounting for phenomena within his own culture. We should like to broaden his concept of myth to include any account of the world, whatever its origin.

For our part, we are in the process of myth making, in furnishing you with an explanation for decision making in education. We take the view that the concept of science, regardless of any notion of truth or accuracy, may be as subject to the process of myth as any account from other explanatory systems: mystical, artistic, religious, political, popular, or 'primitive'. In describing a scientific fact as a myth, we are simply stating that the reason for that piece of knowledge may have a lot to do with power relationships, with who knows what, with who has the rights to that piece of knowledge. Human knowledge is a social phenomenon. It is concerned with communication and cannot be divorced from the regulation of social interaction.

Rituals and routines

Our use of the terms 'rituals' and 'routines' is much more in line with the everyday usage and need take little space by way of explanation. Routines are those aspects of daily or regular practice that are done because that's the way the business gets done. Every morning, a shopkeeper may set out the display of vegetables on the pavement in the same way that he has done for years. Asked why he does it that way, he says that he needs the extra space, but, pushed a little further, he declares that they catch the customer's eye and that the arrangement enables shoppers to look over the produce without being directly under the shopkeeper's scrutiny.

Similarly, the teachers in a school might blow the whistle in the playground twice. The first blast stops all the movement and noise. The second blast is a signal for the children to line up. Questioned about this routine, teachers state that is how they remember lining up as children, that it stops chaos, that it enables teachers to be heard and, as one enquires further, it marks a clear distinction between the freedom of the playground and the more sober activity of the classroom.

Routines, then, are the accepted ways of doing things which lend a sense of order and purpose to daily life. The difference between personal routines (which we all establish as ways of getting up, preparing meals, setting out to work, and so on) and collective organizational routines (as in a school or a factory), is that the collective routines need agreement, explicitly or implicitly, to work. If it is decided that people should walk on the right in corridors, only go up some stairs and down other stairs, go in through one entrance and out through another, then rules are needed. These serve as reminders for people new to the organization, and help in the process of making decisions about sanctions, if any, for those who do not conform.

Our interest in routines is not centred on traffic flow, although as behavioural scientists we are aware of the importance of such seemingly trivial phenomena in determining some of the conflict in schools. We are interested in the explanations that are given about why particular routines are followed. If we asked you, or you asked us, about daily personal routines, we might find it hard to give an explanation, or the explanation would spill over into our next topic, rituals. On the whole, thank goodness, we do not have to account for our daily idiosyncrasies. But when we conform to routine practice as part of an organization, there has to be some explanation of why we do things the way that we do.

It may be that the explanation offered helps support a subcultural myth within the organization. 'It's no good asking why we do things the way we do. You're supposing there's someone in charge who knows what we are supposed to be doing!'. Peters and Waterman (1982) refer to the NETMA phenomenon – No one Ever Tells Me Anything – as an indication of reduced motivation in organizations. To avoid an informational vacuum, explanations are needed for routines.

Rituals, like routines, are individual or collective practices, and again it is the symbolic function of the latter that interests us. There is an element of ceremony about a ritual. It is practice that cannot be explained in everyday terms of commonsense and this marks it off from most routines. Routines have to be accepted for the everyday running of the business. Rituals perform a function for the organization, to do with values, with cohesion, with membership, with definition.

Some rituals are not unusual and simply celebrate some aspect of the organization's work. Graduation ceremonies and other award-giving occasions are obvious examples. Less obvious rituals are sending the recent school-leaver, in his first job, to the stores for a pound of elbow grease, or a long weight. These are part of the initiation rites into work. Again, we are less concerned with the informal rituals that occur in the staffroom or on the shopfloor, than with the rituals that are promoted or sanctioned by the organization. Rituals are a way of understanding the values of the organization.

Suppose we consider the annual ceremony when children are given certificates and prizes for their work and contribution to school. In one school, the ceremony is called Speech Day, even though it is held in the evening. Staff, who are so entitled, are expected to wear academic gowns including hoods, and there is an order to the ceremony which includes all the parents and students standing as the Guest of Honour, headteacher, and staff enter the hall. You can fill in the rest of the details for yourself. In another school, the ceremony is called the Annual Presentation of Awards. The evening provides coffee for the parents, an opportunity to look at exhibitions of children's work, and a presentation ceremony, which is interwoven with a number of short performances of music, poetry, and dance. Dress is not academically formal and presentations are made for all aspects of school life, not just academic and sporting. Again you can add to this second scenario.

It requires no underlining from us to point out how these two ceremonies demonstrate that rituals can reveal something of the values of schools. There is, of course, a shading of routine into ritual and vice versa. A school always plays music at the end of assembly as class by class the students depart. Routine argues that the music covers the otherwise empty waiting period and either reduces or masks talking, hubbub, and possible disorder. Ritual argues that the music creates an atmosphere of worship, of ceremony, of inner calm. Perhaps there is a case for arguing that routine and ritual are distinguishable according to the explanations that are offered. The more the explanation appeals to underlying values, the more the event takes on the appearance of ritual.

What we are arguing, in presenting the importance of myth, ritual, and routine, is that so much of the practice of an organization is socially constructed. Schools, education departments, the Department of Education and Science, universities, nurseries, and classrooms, are all institutions whose practice is socially constructed. These practices are explained by their practitioners and the explanations or accounts are themselves myths, in the sense that we have described the word.

Before we look in more detail at some of the myths in education, let us look at two examples of the way that social forces can shape, or indeed sustain, institutions. Our first example is from R.D. Laing:

> 'Can I help you?' says the patient in a locked back ward to the nurse, who is carrying a pile of laundry to take along to the laundry room.
>
> 'I know what you're after. You just stay where you are. You've been out enough today,' snaps the nurse, as she unlocks the door with her key and slams it behind her.
>
> Staff are 'institutionalized' along with the patients.
>
> I could see the necessity for regimentation and routine, the way rules and roles have to be to make the system work. But I began to question the necessity of that sort of regime.
>
> In hospitals and in mental hospitals and in in-patient psychiatric units where biorhythm is under surveillance, and control, this power of control over the biorhythm of patients usually takes the form of regimentation. That is, it has to do with doing things at the same time; the 'ward' has to be in bed, silent, asleep, up, eat the same food, at the same time. A lot of medication is required to keep up this regimentation. Patients have to be drugged to sleep, and drugged to keep awake.
>
> (Laing 1985:26)

The second observation on the procedure of an institution is from Rom Harré in conversation with Jonathan Miller In *States of Mind*, in which Harré states:

> Institutions exist day by day and year by year. It is curious, isn't it, that there might be a night on which every member of Oxford University was fast asleep, yet the next day up we get and a recognizably similar institution exists again. I think that we ought to be amazed that this kind of thing is possible. How can it be that we recreate an institution over and over again, surviving wars and pestilence, kings' commissioners, and innumerable changes of personnel? There must be something that outlasts these changes. These are the overlapping systems of rules, or something approximating to them, some normative entity that is like a system of rules. This idea is the central 'as if', the one I take to be crucial to the scientific study of the human mind in action.
>
> (Miller 1983)

Of course, you might want to point out that both Oxford University and the psychiatric hospital have formal rules and that these are available for inspection. What is of interest here is the process of

83

control. This process carries on even though most of the people engaged in the reconstruction have no idea of the formal rules. The rules, despite being formal and laid down in some dusty archive, have survived and have been transmitted to the inmates of the institutions. These rules are now manifest in the manner in which those people within the institution conform to them. They have become social rules. New members of these organizations will learn 'the ropes', will be indoctrinated into the way things get done. Apart from the constitutional, formal rules, there will be a whole host of informal rules to learn.

What Harré finds marvellous is the way that the institution as a social event is reconstructed on a daily basis, reconstructed one might say by the interweaving of the behavioural patterns of the individuals within the institution. It 'teaches' the individual how to behave and continues to function as an institution because the individual carries out this new behaviour. No wonder institutions exert such a control over people. They need to do so in order to survive. Naturally, there is a process of interaction between the individual and the institution and it is in this way, among others, that change occurs. Not all institutions are as immutable as psychiatric hospitals and universities!

In view of the power that the social construction of our world possesses to resurrect institutions on a daily basis, or to develop patterns of behaviour that would, in other contexts, be considered odd if not insane, it is not surprising that strong explanations are necessary to justify practice. It is from these justifications that we identify myths.

Let us now turn to some of the myths that exist in education, remembering that our view of them is that they are accounts, given by members of educational institutions as explanations of organizational or individual practices and that the practices that they support may be routines or rituals.

The myth that education matters

Perhaps the first issue that gives rise to myths is the one concerning the importance of education itself. During the 1960s, under the Wilson government, there was an upsurge in the view that education could be a tool of social change. By increasing educational opportunity, some of the inequalities of wealth and privilege would be nullified. Peter Mortimore and his former colleagues in the ILEA Research and Statistics Department chose for their longitudinal study of nearly 2,000 school children in primary schools, the title, *School Matters* (Mortimore *et al.* 1988). In this study, they identified the factors in the organization and management of primary schools that appear to affect pupil outcomes. They also looked at whether schools had a differential effect on children from manual and non-manual families. They state:

Overall, therefore, we found that there was little difference in the size of the effects of individual schools on the progress of children from different social class groups. Those schools which were effective for one group tended to be effective for the other. Conversely, those which were ineffective for one group were also usually ineffective for the other. Our results show, therefore, that effective schools tend to 'jack up' the progress of all pupils, irrespective of their social class background, while ineffective schools will usually depress the progress of all pupils.

(Mortimore 1988:209)

Ivan Reid (1988) looks at the results of studies concerned with whether education can influence social class. He points out that most of the evidence shows that 'educational outcomes tend, in general, to reflect or reproduce existing social stratifications in our society, albeit with relatively small variations'.

Looking at the question of whether schools matter, in the sense of whether they can influence the educational differences of pupils from different social classes, the answer seems to be that they cannot. Mortimore *et al.* note that Rutter (1983) states that if all schools become more effective, the results would be an overall improvement in standards, rather than a removal of deeply rooted social class differences in educational standards. This view represents a blow to those politicians and educators who hoped to see, through education, the reduction in social class disadvantage.

What the results of studies such as those of Rutter and Mortimore perhaps show, is that to produce a differential effect, positive discrimination in favour of socially disadvantaged pupils is necessary. The educational practice of positive discrimination would require educationalists to promote those values that bring about equal opportunity, or at least to respond to the lead of politicians with those values. Indeed, this is what has happened and many local authorities, not only Labour authorities, have pursued an equal opportunities policy that actively discriminates in favour of certain groups. These results tell us a lot about the pervasiveness of social class differences in our society, when the application of better education will not remove the stratification.

Although we have put forward some views that education is unable to combat social inequalities, this does not mean that we have successfully undermined the myth that education matters. There can be other ways of judging the value of education than measuring its influence in social engineering terms. As we write, there seems to be a movement to demystify education. Attempts to describe education in quite simple terms of what it produces, by using performance indicators, might even be reflected in the move towards testing and assessment.

If education is seen as being uncomplicated, if it is simply a matter of measuring output, then these views pave the way for opinions such as that teachers do not need to be trained in teaching, at least not in any theoretical framework, that tests of standards of performance are easy to construct, and that a structured National Curriculum is easily described. People holding these views are not saying that such education does not matter. It could be argued, however, that they are saying that much of what other people regard as education does not matter.

The myth of falling standards

What lies behind some of these ideas is yet another myth – that educational standards have fallen. The emphasis on educational targets, narrowing the focus to the basic parts of the curriculum, is based on the myth that there has been a decline in educational performance. In commenting here, we are not saying that standards have or have not fallen. Both views are myths. They may or may not be supported by evidence, that is not the point. Readers looking for a review of the evidence might look at Brian Simon's book *Bending the Rules* (1988).

What the arguments about standards represent are rallying points for people with opposing values. Arthur Combs quotes the following: 'Whenever you find an idea that can be expressed as either–or, it is almost certain they are both wrong' (Combs 1979:3). We are not concerned with the rightfulness or wrongfulness of the idea, so much as what the idea stands for. It does seem rather surprising, however, that standards should have all risen or all fallen over a given period. It is much more likely that improvements have been made in some areas of the curriculum and not in others. Indeed, it would be quite difficult to measure the progress of the educational system as a whole through a single statistic. For example, is the final point of output the number of exam successes at sixteen years? Or should the results at eighteen be added to the picture? Perhaps, if students are given a broader, but less academically excellent, secondary education, the effects are measurable at a later stage, say at twenty-one years.

Another question concerns how one sums up the different exam results. Are the efforts of getting a Grade B instead of a Grade C, the same as getting an A instead of a B? How does one interpret the statistic, for example, that in one year 15 per cent received Grade A and 30 per cent received Grade B, and the next year, 12 per cent received an A Grade and 36 per cent received a B? Did standards fall? How do you make sense of those sort of data, especially across lots of subjects, across lots of examination boards, even until recently, across two major examinations? One answer has to be that the evidence cannot resolve the differences between adversaries. It is a question of belief, of values, and in this situation the scope for myth is enormous.

If yet more evidence or argument is required to illustrate the power of myth, consider the notion that the National Curriculum was introduced to raise educational standards. The myth of educational decline was sufficiently powerful to propel a government to enact legislation that has substantially altered the framework of teaching in this country. That such a major change can be introduced without a consensual acceptance of evidence that there was need for such change is a testament to the power of the myth.

The myth of the industrial clone

There were, of course, other arguments also leading to the 1988 Education Act. There was the view that education was not delivering what employers wanted in the way of skills among school-leavers. What did employers want? The myth was that they wanted youngsters who could read, write, spell, total up a column of figures, in short have the same skills as previous generations. Was there evidence that school-leavers were not able to do these things as well as their elders? Were schools and industrialists not talking to each other about the skills of school-leavers? We would be most surprised if industry did not want young people with originality, creativity, enthusiasm, the ability to problem-solve, to think laterally, to make connections, and to innovate. What have been the changes between generations in respect of these skills and how will they be tackled within the National Curriculum?

A myth, or a collection of myths, has lead to and created the climate for enormous change. The pursuit of an accountancy approach to education has meant that there has been an attempt, on the one hand, to measure effectiveness or benefits through the establishment of a National Curriculum and assessment of children, and, on the other hand, through local financial management, to apply measures of cost. In this way a cost-benefit equation can be applied. The myth of educational inefficiency has spawned all sorts of new practices in education. Headteachers have become financial managers, and advisers have become educational auditors.

The myth of parental involvement

Another myth that has prompted considerable change is the notion that parents want more say in their children's education, particularly in the choice of school and, through the changes in the composition of governing bodies, in the running of the school. Yet again, we would remind the reader that in saying that parental involvement is a myth, we do not imply that it is not true, or even that it has been exaggerated. What we do mean is that the concept of parental involvement has become a vehicle for the expression of values. The promulgation of the myth has paved the way for change. It has permitted the central government to limit some of the power of local government in the name of parental power.

The myth of competition

One of the major societal myths that Combs (1979) addresses is that of the competitive society. He argues that much educational practice in the United States is based on the notion of competition and its value in fitting young people to life after school. He maintains, however, that the attribute most commonly employed by people in all aspects of their interactions is that of co-operation and that it is this skill that we should be teaching. As a myth, the need for competitiveness in education has come to the fore in this country too.

By setting the available places in schools at a level based on a historic figure, the government is seeking to increase parental choice of secondary school. Local authorities will not be able to limit the numbers of children to levels determined by, for example, the number of teachers, and within the limits of safe accommodation, schools will be obliged to admit children up to the designated figure. With the move towards publication of the results of assessments, it is likely that some schools that are less popular will get fewer pupils. Hence, at a stroke, the government has set the scene for inter-school competition.

What will now become important to schools if they wish to retain or increase their pupil numbers? Good local press reports? Low levels of disruption? High academic progress as measured by examination results? What will be bad news for such schools will be the presence of disaffected pupils and those with learning difficulties. The 1986 Education Act has made it easier to remove children by exclusion. Following the implementation of that Act, headteachers, when they excluded children, became accountable largely to their governors and less to panels of officers and members. Similarly, under the Regulations of the 1988 Act, appeals by parents, when their children have been denied access to the National Curriculum, will be heard by the governors. It is likely that the interests of the governors and those of the schools will be similar. Who will speak for those students who do not fit into the school mould?

The myth of competitiveness may well serve to increase uniformity among schools in terms of what they offer – where will be the school that used to put its emphasis on good pastoral care, for instance – and to increase conformity among students. Yet again, a view about human nature, or in this case, about the value of market forces in education, has had a direct effect on practice.

Some other myths briefly visited

A senior parliamentary politician asked a group of psychologists why they did so little to tackle the problems of delinquents and criminals at an early age. The politician had been told by an experienced nursery headteacher, that she could spot future criminals during their time in her nursery school. The Member of Parliament wanted to know why psychologists did not get to work on such children right away. What a wonderful way to develop a myth! No doubt the parliamentarian in question has continued to have confidence in the value of nursery education on the grounds that it could be an opportunity for the screening of the population to find criminals.

This introduces us to the myth of early development. Clarke and Clarke (1976) wrote a book entitled *Early Experience: Myth and Evidence*. We have reservations about the title. It presupposes that there is a contrast to be made between myth and evidence, whereas we see myths as being accounts of the world whether evidential or otherwise. However, what the authors achieved was to call into question many of the assumptions about the uniqueness of early experience. In part, their message was a plea for professionals and others to not give up on older children because of unfounded beliefs about early critical periods for child development. Since that book, Barbara Tizard (1988) and others have looked at the value of early education and begun to tease out which aspects seem to be relevant to future educational progress.

The whole area of early childhood education remains, none the less, surrounded by myths. Yet again we would attribute these myths to people who do not wish to argue at the level of values but to pretend that the arguments are about more superficial matters. For instance, there is a view that children should not be taught to read too early, which suggests shades of the Piagetian critical period concept. Parents are told not to engage in any teaching of reading to their children before they start school.

Barbara Tizard is uncommon among early education experts in this country in recognizing that early education skills *are* taught by parents, and that children with such skills at admission to primary school tend to do better than children without such skills. Educationalists in cultures as diverse as the USSR and the USA do see the need for early intervention of an educational nature as a way of breaking into the problems of disadvantage. As long as children are strung out by the process of education along a continuum of have and have-not, children that start primary education disadvantaged are most likely to stay that way. The availability of diffuse, non-compensatory provision, such as nursery education, will have no effect on disadvantage. What are needed are target programmes of intervention that recognize the special educative role of the adult, be it parent or teacher – but this is another myth to which we are contributing!

What are the other frequently encountered myths in education? Well, there's the myth about the size of the teaching group. 'When you get to that number, you can only entertain them, not teach them!' Again, there is an echo of a discussion in an earlier chapter about the need for individualized teaching. The issue of teaching children as individuals relates to the issue of teaching large groups. Like so many issues in education, there is controversy about the evidence, and this is not a debate that will be easily settled by reference to evidence. For one thing, the measures of outcome will vary from activity to activity and, as with myths surrounding teaching methods, there may be no grounds for supposing any one answer is always right. So consistent has been the teacher union lobby on this issue, however, that the Elton Committee of Enquiry into discipline in schools acknowledged that teachers reported that large class sizes contributed to the difficulties of classroom management.

Another myth is that when the teacher first encounters a new group, she 'must not smile till Christmas', that is, she must establish who is boss before easing up and getting closer to the children. Perhaps this is part of the competitive myth and a view of children as a group 'being out to get you', or, possibly, the view that familiarity breeds contempt. Whatever the data for these views, they do say a lot about one perspective of the role of the teacher – the teacher as lion-tamer. Combs talks about the 'attack–appease' myth, the view that the alternative to attack is appeasement. He suggests that there is scope for what he refers to as 'the humane approach', whereby we take a strong neutral position and he likens it to the views of Schweitzer and Gandhi.

There is a myth which is not confined to education. We might refer to it as the 'if only' myth. It goes like this:

> 'if only I didn't have those two in my class'
> 'if only his parents took some interest in him'
> 'if only I had some more free periods'
> 'if only I didn't have this Christmas play to produce'

Add your own to the list! What this myth is about is that the problem is outside your control or power. In a later chapter we shall look at ritual encounters that form part of games that people play. Berne (1964) describes the game of 'Ain't it awful'. 'If only' might be its stable mate. As a myth it limits one's capacity for tackling a situation by placing the locus of control in another system – it's the headteacher's or parent's or student's or local authority's or government's fault. But such an account has functional value as do all myths, routines, and rituals. It might take some pressure off you to blame someone else and providing you don't get hooked on that explanation but can tackle the really manageable parts of the problem when you have got your breath back, perhaps there is no harm in the myth. The real danger is that myths can be so convenient as explanations for complex events that we opt out of taking a more critical and challenging view.

Let us summarize our theme at this point. Routines occur in organizations, as well as in our personal lives, because we are creatures of habit, because that's the way the business has always been done, because that's how everyone else does it, or because that's the way it has been agreed. Rituals occur as a more deliberate way of celebrating or otherwise marking some feature of the organization. Rituals can occur in our personal behaviour and may be anxiety-reducing, or stimulating, or in some way serve our needs. In the organization, a ritual is related to the values of that organization. Myths are the explanations that we use to justify or account for our practice. Myths belong to groups of people. Those that subscribe to, retell, or add to the myth demonstrate their membership of the group.

Myths, traditionally based on hearsay, may now be based on so-called scientific evidence. They are not right or wrong. They serve many purposes. One purpose is to permit people to identify each other as belonging to a group, without having to declare more fundamental values. If I retell a story concerning an ethnic group, I identify myself and seek out others who might identify with me, without declaring my prejudicial values. The teacher in the classroom will encounter, and will also subscribe to, many myths. It is our view that there are unlikely to be myth-free social situations. But by recognizing that a particular view is a myth, is about group identity, is about exploring unstated common values, the teacher is in a stronger position to relate myths, routines, and rituals to her own value system. In this way, she is able to question not only practices, but the explanation of practices.

Chapter Seven

Making language work

Language has enormous power to permit each of us to reconstruct
reality, or fantasy, to depict history from a time before people, to
imagine the future, to plan, to describe, to communicate our innermost
feelings and thoughts, and to examine the very nature of language itself.
The ideas in this book are conveyed entirely by language. Because they
are printed and not spoken, they may be stored for as long as the book
retains its physical integrity and legibility. The ideas may also, we hope,
interact with the views of the reader, so that they are taken forward and
are passed on orally or in writing for others to use. Apart from our
obvious wonder at language, what reasons do we have for devoting a
chapter of this book to it?

The book, so far, has explored the themes of influences on teachers
and how teachers can steer an accountable and yet independent course
in their professional practice. Justifying at the simplest level our interest
in language, we can point out that the processes that we have discussed
so far – curriculum perspectives, myths, rituals and routines, personal
identities, power relationships, and hidden messages – are all dependent
on language for their maintenance and communication.

Our interest in language, however, extends beyond its obvious
involvement in the processes of influence. Language is not just the oil
that lubricates the cogs of social interaction and private thought. It is not
neutral, not an impartial device for communicating and thinking. It is, in
our view, locked into these processes themselves. Choosing words,
consciously or otherwise, is neither an accidental, nor an incidental, part
of communicating.

Language in teaching

Education is about communicating, about influencing the development
of people, about shaping the ideas and the behaviour of future generations by the previous generations. Education relies heavily on
language, not only as an integral part of the teaching process, but also as

a means of controlling the content, methods, and values conveyed in that process. Since communicating is the very stuff of teaching and education, the use of language in that sphere is of specific interest to us and deserves close scrutiny.

Suppose that you are required to teach some aspect of engineering or cookery. If you reflect for a moment, you will recognize what sort of an activity this is. You are required to transmit some part of your culture, something that you know, to others. Apart from focusing on the engineering task or the cookery task itself in your preparation for the lesson, you will also need to teach the language of engineering or cookery, as far as these are necessary for the particular item to be taught. You might need to describe, for example, the process of basting and the use of a basting spoon, or describe a flange and its purpose in the particular machine assembly that you are examining. There is thus a technical language component to what the student must learn.

The next component of language in this teaching process is the language of instruction. Apart from the technical and specialized vocabulary of engineering or cookery, you will use language which is specific to the teaching situation. The phrases that you use will mark the fact that you are the teacher and the students are learners, for example:

'I want you to look very closely at this part'
'Now, can anyone tell me why it is that ...'

These phrases are unusual phrases, not the substance of everyday communication, but they are conventional, in the sense that the students expect you to talk like that when you are in the teaching mode. If you try this style as, say, a parent, you are likely to occasion groans and the glazing over of eyes that parents get when they try deliberately to adopt a didactic role with their children. In the workshop, in the home economics room, in the classroom, there is an acceptance of the instructional language mode. The tone of voice, the directness of questions and of instructions, and the proportion of the interaction taken by you as the teacher will be acceptable in this context. Teachers are sometimes accused of continuing these aspects of language into other social settings, a source of annoyance or amusement to others, but then the same charge might be levelled at other workers, who take a mode of language away from the workplace into other contexts.

As a teacher of engineering or cookery, you have to use the technical language of your subject and the language of teaching or instruction. The language of instruction will reflect speech that is used commonly by all teachers and which reflects a particular teaching style. However, a cookery teacher or a CDT teacher might also use a style common to teachers who have to manage practical subjects, where, for example, dangers are present and so routines are necessary. The language of explaining about lighting a gas jet or a blow-torch might be considerably more directive than the language of considering the origins of the First World War.

Much of the language that you use in the teaching situation is, none the less, your individual language. This is your language of inter-personal style. It will change from situation to situation, but there is a consistency which represents you. Unless you are a capable of putting on a complete act, your interpersonal style is your own and is present in every social situation in which you take part. The language you use conveys a great deal of information to those with whom you engage in conversation.

Personal language style

Let us consider some of the information that your personal language conveys to others. In so doing, let us also suppose that the following process is involved in your interaction with another person:

—— What you mean to say
—— How you manage to say what you mean
—— What the other person thinks you will say
—— What the other person thinks you said
—— What the other person thinks you meant

In commenting on this process, we are also making lots of guesses as to what is going on, and so when we talk about looking at the information that your personal language conveys, we ought to remind ourselves that we are making an interpretation too.

One of the authors recalls watching a group of children working with their teacher on recording the colour of cars owned by the families of the children. The results had been displayed on a bar chart. The teacher asked the children to think of questions that they could ask about the chart. The first two respondents asked questions of the 'how many' variety – 'how many families had brown cars?'. The third respondent asked a different question – 'why did so many families buy red or white or silver cars?'. 'Oh!' laughed the teacher, 'that's not something we can work out from the chart. Has anyone else got another question?' The third child looked a little embarrassed, aware that, somehow, he'd missed the point. In fact, the teacher probably had not realized that her request to the class was more open-ended than she had intended. The child had not read what was in the teacher's mind. The result was that the child had entered fully into the spirit of enquiry, but had not asked a numerical question. Nevertheless, he learned a very important lesson about life. Adults have the power to move the goal posts.

Another point that needs to be made is that language can convey information over and above that which is conveyed by the content. How you talk is part of your self-presentation, part of the data on which others attempt to predict you, and on which they can base their interaction with you. (In addition, of course, there are non-verbal factors, such as your clothes, your movements, your facial expression, that are all part of the way that you are 'interpreted' by others. Some of the accounts of classroom management, for example, have recognized the importance of some of the non-verbal signals in helping teachers assume status and control among groups of students.)

Your accent, your use of certain phrases and vocabulary, your voice tone, your use of pauses, your speech hesitations, will all combine to convey your relative status. People with whom you converse may draw inferences about the group or subgroup to which you belong. They will judge how you feel about the situation, whether you are confident or hesitant, on top of the job or struggling, interested or bored, involved or detached. They will make judgements about whether you are easy to approach, whether you like them, whether you are enjoying yourself, whether you are predictable.

All of these processes will be in operation as well as the actual content of your lesson. Apart from what you *mean* to convey about the matter in hand, there will be all these other signals available to be interpreted. There may be aspects, as well, that arise from the agendas of your students, which influence how they view and interpret the situation:

> 'Will the teacher be giving us homework tonight? I want to go out with my mates this evening.'
> 'Shall I tell the teacher that I've lost my book now, or wait till later?'
> 'I wonder why Mum was in such a bad mood this morning. Was it my fault?'

These influences, that impinge on the student, may affect what the student understands of your lesson. They may affect how the student sees you or responds to the interaction. In whatever ways you seek to control the language and your own self-presentation, the meaning that is abstracted from the interaction depends, in part, on the interpretation from the other person. This does not absolve us, however, from having a direct responsibility for the way in which we use language. Language conveys so much of what we think, not only about the topic of conversation, but also about the person with whom we are talking, that it would be naïve to pay no regard to its influence.

We shall argue at a later point that communication, by its very nature, is liable to engender misinterpretations and that to disregard the likelihood of this happening is to contribute to interpersonal tension and conflict.

Straight and crooked talking

There are, of course, people who make a living out of paying attention to language by polishing up the way that their clients present themselves. Elocution is available for those who feel that their speech affects adversely their social or professional development. It may be that there is a specific problem about the way in which you present that obscures what you mean. To deal with such an obstacle is, no doubt, sensible.

There are, however, other practitioners of the art of communication whose business is concerned less with making accessible what their clients wish to say, and more with developing wider powers of influence over audiences. One of our interests in this chapter is to look at aspects of language that obscure meaning, to bring those aspects forward for consideration, and to emphasize throughout that, for each of us, the moral position is to strive for understanding, not to use language to manipulate or deceive. Our emphasis on paying attention to the language of interaction is towards a greater understanding of interpersonal processes. Language can be used for effect. Politicians and other public speakers employ language devices in their speech that enhance the emphasis of what they want to say and that win greater acceptance from their audience.

This has been strikingly illustrated by both Atkinson (1984) and Heritage and Greatbach (1986). They have drawn attention to specific techniques used by politicians to earn applause during their speeches. One of the most effective relates to the use of inversions. A much quoted example is President Kennedy's request to Americans in the 1960s: 'Ask not what your country can do for you but what you can do for your country'. During the 1987 UK general election campaign, Neil Kinnock, leader of the Labour Party declared, 'I will die for my country, but I will not let my country die for me'. A more notorious example, from one of Hollywood's wittiest women, Mae West, was, 'It's not the men in my life that matters, but the life in my men'.

Apart from the influence over audiences that can be achieved by the manipulation of the form of one's sentences, there are many ways in which illegitimate influence can be gained by arguments themselves. Robert Thouless (1974) wrote a book entitled *Straight and Crooked Thinking* in 1930, which remains a classic in describing illegitimate argument. In the appendix of that book, Thouless lists thirty-eight dishonest tricks of argument together with his suggestions for dealing with them. For example, his fourth point is referred to as extension of an opponent's proposition by contradiction or misrepresentation of it (p. 193).

In the body of the text, Thouless explains how, in the course of a discussion, it is possible for one person (A) to take an extreme position. The second person (B) might win the argument by remaining reasonable. However, if B is persuaded to respond in kind by countering the wild claims by equally wild claims, then A can score by simply attacking the first unsupportable wild claim made by B. For example, let us suppose the following conversation occurs:

(A) 'What with all these modern approaches in education, no wonder standards are falling!'
(B) 'I don't think that is true.'
(A) 'Discipline is non-existent and more and more children are leaving school totally illiterate because of these child-centred approaches.'
(B) 'That's rubbish! Standards are rising.'
(A) 'If that's the case, how do you explain the report from HMI on literacy standards on young people entering the Employment Training scheme?'

This short fictitious exchange suffices to illustrate that B was drawn into making sweeping generalizations and was left exposed. It also illustrates another dishonest trick described by Thouless as 'proof by selected instances'. In the scenario, A refers to one report as a means of upholding the claim that standards are falling. Interested readers are recommended to read Thouless to supplement this short example.

Manipulative language

Language is not just open to misinterpretation, therefore. It can be deliberately manipulated to exert influence over the way others understand it. An example of this manipulation of language can be found in an advert placed in *The Guardian* newspaper (17 September 1988), in which the Tobacco Advisory Council reproduced three extracts from three other newspapers describing accounts of actual physical aggression towards the police in quite graphic details:

'WPC beaten senseless as 60 cheer'
'Black and blue line: 50 police are beaten up every day of the year'
'Hero Cop Shot. He tackled bank gang'

Then the advert quotes from another newspaper story:

'and to add insult to injury ...
Ban on Police Smokes
Smoking became a criminal offence today as far as some
policemen were concerned. They are now banned from lighting
up at their stations and in patrol cars.'

The final point made by the Tobacco Advisory Council states:

'After the bricks, bottles and bullets, shouldn't the police be
spared the attentions of the anti-smoking lobby?'

By implication, the anti-smoking lobby's views are associated with
the decision to end smoking in some sections of the police force. By
further implication, the anti-smoking lobby is associated with some of
the violence towards the police. One way of reading the final remark is
as follows: 'After the bricks, bottles, bullets of the anti-smoking lobby
shouldn't the police be spared its attentions?'

We accept that this is merely one interpretation, but the case for
leaving poor bobbies to have their smokes in peace is that they have
already had to face such harrowing violence. 'If you deplore the
violence towards the police you will also deplore this restriction', seems
to be the message of the advert. The issue of concern here is not the
arguments for and against smoking but whether the association of ideas
is a legitimate communication or one which seeks to use undue
influence in changing the opinion of others.

Let us leave that example to make a general point. The reader might
consider that we are taking a very harsh attitude in ascribing intention-
ality to the words that are used in communication. Words convey a
complexity of meanings which are dependent upon the context and the
nature of the discourse, among many factors, in order for any precision
to be achieved. Is it reasonable to hold individuals responsible for the
interpretations of their words that others place upon them? Is not the
receiver also responsible for the interpretation? Might not some people
deliberately, or unwittingly, misinterpret the communications of others?

In the example above, where the communication is carefully
prepared with a conscious intention of producing an effect upon the
reader, it seems not unreasonable to place the onus for the interpretation
of the message on the sender. But what about spontaneous conversation
between people in the course of their everyday communications? Do we
always have to assume single-handed responsibility for the course of the
communication, for the effectiveness of the message?

One of the authors recalls how, as a newly qualified teacher, he was
drawn into debates, not unwillingly, with the headteacher, who, while
seeking discussion on educational issues with someone straight from
college, used to get quite heated. On such occasions, he would say, 'You

people ... you come in here with your theories ...!' More recently, this author heard an item on the radio concerning a commissioned report on the Metropolitan Police Force in which the firm of consultants had drawn attention to a few police officers whose attitude to the public was not acceptable. The spokesman, a senior officer, had commented that 'these people' needed to be identified and evidence acquired in order to be able to proceed properly with their dismissal. By using the terms 'You people' and 'these people', both the headteacher and the police spokesman were seeking to establish a category. For the one, the category might have consisted of 'wet-behind-the-ears-straight-from-college-full-of-ideas-and-no-experience-probationary-teachers'. For the other, the category might have been 'officers-who-let-the-side-down-and-give-the-force-a-bad-name'. The impression that is given in both cases is that there are categories into which it is useful to place individuals and to which you can ascribe attributes belonging to all the people who are included in that category.

Our view is that speakers, and particularly writers, are responsible for the choice of words. If the writer pleads that her or his intention was different from the message as received, then she or he must bear the responsibility for the ambiguity of the message. Speakers are responsible for checking what the hearers understand of their communication, although as we shall mention later, listeners also have a responsibility to check out their understanding.

One further point about language is that it is a basis for thinking. It may be argued that, as well as taking care in their external communication, individuals should be careful with the language that they use to think with, in that if they get into the habit of thinking with language that is careless, overladen with bias, or prejudicial, then it will be much harder to engage in an open discussion with others.

The language of control

The previous section has drawn attention to the ways that language can be used to influence people, in terms of both the style of presentation and the arguments put forward. Let us now turn to some of the ways that language can be used in a variety of situations as a means of control. We begin by looking at the way that language can be a mechanism for controlling culture. Michael Sheridan in *The Independent*, writing about Archbishop Lefebvre of the Catholic Church, described some of the aspects of the archbishop's practice that marked him out as ultra-conservative and in opposition to the main body of the Church:

> In its place, his followers celebrate the so-called Tridentine Mass codified by Pope Pius V, a solemn and mystical Latin rite. 'The

fact that Latin is a dead language,' observes the archbishop, 'is in its favour. It is the best means of protecting the expression of faith against linguistic changes which come about naturally in the course of time.'

(The Independent, 30 June 1988)

Archbishop Lefebvre has a clear idea of the power of language. If you fail to halt its progress, then concepts that can only be enshrined linguistically become eroded as words that have been used in their description begin to take on new meaning. From this, it can be seen that concepts are inseparable from the language used to express them. This gives rise to a number of linguistic and communicative problems. Not only does the meaning of words change, as the archbishop points out, but also the meaning of words can vary from situation to situation and from individual to individual. And yet it might be that this process of change is all part of human progress and that it mainly poses problems for someone with fixed views rather than for others.

Yet another example of control is to be found in relation to knowledge. The social psychologist, Rom Harré, in a conversation with Miller makes the following comment:

> Knowledge is never stationary. There is a kind of seepage. Knowledge is moving through society all the time. If we think of knowledge as socially located, it can start its social journey in highly technical institutions, an esoteric knowledge known only to a few. But soon it begins to leak away and permeate the whole of society.

(Miller 1983:66)

In this extract, Harré is talking not about language as such, but the process of 'seepage' might very well be associated with language. It is probable that the conceptual or scientific advances made within the highly technical institutions are conveyed to others more by language than, for example, by the spy's photographs. This permeation of knowledge through society does pose problems, none the less, and not only for those who want some aspects of the world to stand still. The problem is to do with the use of language as the method of conveying meaning.

Language and the control of meaning

In a conversation with Bryan Magee, John Searle makes the following observation about Wittgenstein's views on meaning:

> In his later work, he abandoned the picture theory of meaning in favour of a use or tool conception of meaning. He urges us to think of words as tools, think of sentences as instruments. To get a

correct conception of language we need simply to look at how it functions in real life, we need to look at what people do with words. He says, 'for a large class of cases – though not for all – in which we employ the word "meaning" it can be defined thus: the meaning of a word is its use in the language.'

(Magee 1987:326)

If we take this point about the meaning of a word being determined by its use, then Wittgenstein sets us some more problems. In his *Philosophical Investigations* (Wittgenstein 1984), he writes 'Language is a labyrinth of paths. You approach from *one* side and know your way about; you approach the same place from another side and no longer know your way about'. (Wittgenstein 1984:203)

Meanings of words are not absolutely and permanently defined but are interpreted according to the way they are used. The way words are used is, according to Wittgenstein, illuminated by the particular 'language game' within which they are employed. By language game, he meant the type of discourse in which people are engaged. Thus there might be a scientific language game; a theological language game; a psychological language game; and so on. These language games might share some word usage with or without the same meaning. The word 'belief' might have different connotations in psychology and theology.

As interpreters of language, it is necessary for us to recognize these cautionary considerations as we try to extract the fullest meaning from language that we receive from others. Unless we resort to Lefebvre's approach, of using a dead language within a highly ritualized context, we are bound to be expressing ourselves, communicating our views, signalling our emotions, through the medium of a living language. The words of this language are not fixed in their meaning and it is interesting to look at some of the methods that may be used to secure meaning, to anchor it to certain words.

In the fourth book in the Hitch Hiker series by Douglas Adams, there is a particularly relevant passage:

It was a press conference.

'I'm afraid I can't comment on the name Rain God at this present time, and we are calling him an example of a Spontaneous Para-Causal Meteorological Phenomenon.'

'Can you tell us what that means?'

'I'm not altogether sure. Let's be straight here. If we find something we can't understand, we like to call it something you can't understand, or indeed pronounce. I mean, if we just let you go around calling him a Rain God, then that suggests that you know something that we don't, and I'm afraid we couldn't have that.

'No, first we have to call it something which says it's ours, not

101

yours, then we set about finding some way of proving it's not what you said it is, but something we say it is.

'And if it turns out that you are right, you'll still be wrong, because we simply call him a ... er, "Supernormal..." not para-normal or supernatural because you think you know what those mean now, no, a "Supernormal Incremental Precipitation Inducer". We'll probably want to shove in a "Quasi" in there somewhere to protect ourselves. Rain God! Huh, never heard such nonsense in my life. Admittedly, you wouldn't catch me going on holiday with him....'

(Adams 1984)

Here is one fictitious, and, we hope, illuminating way of attempting to control definition. Another example occurred at a seminar at a conference attended by one of the authors. During a dramatic reconstruction of a family therapy session, the term 'resistance' was used. This incensed one of the audience so much that during the discussion, he told the presenters that they had no right to use the term without a full understanding of psychodynamic psychology and should restrict its use to that specific meaning.

Paraphrasing that into Wittgenstein's analysis, one might say that he objected to the removal of a term from the psychodynamic language game, where it properly belonged. No doubt, some student of electrical physics might have objected to the term 'resistance' being in the psychodynamic language game in the first place, and what about a student of political theory or a French historian of the Second World War? There is no doubt that words do migrate from one language game to another, from one type of discourse to another. In so doing, they possibly enrich the concepts of the new game by dragging across something of the concepts of the old game. They may also bring across implications, or overtones of meaning, that do not fit so well into the new game.

Meaning and the education game

Unless, as in the press conference depicted by Douglas Adams, you wish to select words deliberately for their capacity to mystify, any honest attempt to communicate will be bedevilled by the additional unwanted overtones. It is perhaps the combination of words that have partially duplicating overtones, which permits the highly skilled communicator to convey meaning with more precision. It is also possible to want to communicate in a way that is not too precise. Some of the most poetic or stirring writing in a language requires the writer to surprise the reader with choices of words. The use of metaphor can be refreshing; ambiguity can heighten the significance of text as the reader or hearer plays around with the possible meaning. To use language in these ways is to play a different language game. These belong to the creative language game, whereas we are describing the straight communication language game.

This is not to say that metaphor has no place in straight communication. Andrew Wilkinson draws attention to an article by W.J. Cheverst, who describes three groups of metaphors to be found in educational writing. Wilkinson writes:

> In that which is *child-centred* we find words like 'growth', 'harmony', 'discovery', 'assimilation', 'readiness'. In that which is *knowledge-centred* we find words like 'store', 'foundation', 'stock', 'cells', 'bricks', 'structure'. In that which is *teacher-centred* there are words like 'guiding', 'shaping', 'moulding', 'directing', 'imparting'.
>
> (Wilkinson 1975)

It is possible to argue that these metaphors are words that have been taken from other language games, and that as knowledge 'seeps' from one context into another, so does meaning. It is a process that is both enriching and impoverishing, since it can be argued that by using a word out of its specific context, some of its original specificity is lost. That concern for the integrity of meaning was, no doubt, the reason for our colleague's determination that psychodynamics owns the word 'resistance'.

It is not possible to put artificial boundaries around words in this way, but it is not surprising that people attempt to do so. Sharing the specificity of meaning that some words have in some language games provides a form of identity for a group of people. Orthodoxy is very often a linguistic matter. Through the choice of metaphor, individuals communicate to others that their underpinning ideas are similar and, perhaps, conform to some group norm.

All of us involved in the process of education have words that we use, codes that identify us as educationalists. Sometimes these words take the form of initials, particularly infuriating to those not initiated, since without the key, it is impossible to crack the code and one remains on the outside. PTR is one example. TVE is another. Try talking to someone with no connections with education about CPVE, NCC, LEATGS, or PSME. In psychology, the initials are just as difficult – ABA and S-R learning. Is this all about shorthand? Is it simply a matter of those with similar reference points being able to shortcut much of the language in order to concentrate on the bits that convey the real information? That may well be part of it, but there is a less charitable interpretation that this is a form of linguistic protectionism.

Just as we pointed out in relation to the use of legitimate and illegitimate means of influencing the views of others, it is not easy to decide whether the use of particular terms is intended to restrict access to meaning, to close ranks in the face of the outsider, or whether it is a genuine way of assuming common reference points. In practice, it depends on an analysis of the linguistic context, including a study of the interactions prior to the present one.

Negotiating meaning

What we have said about language so far points us towards a specific conclusion. We have indicated that, within the framework of a living language, the meaning of a word is not absolutely clear. It has to be inferred from the context, by reference to the language game that governs the discourse and to the interaction between the parties involved. Another way of putting this is to say that meaning is negotiable. What sense you make of what I say, can only be clarified if you ask me to explain what I mean and, indeed, if I ask you to tell me whether you have understood, or what you have understood. Meaning requires commentary, in the sense of explanation. Wittgenstein wrote:

> If language is to be a means of communication there must be agreement not only in definitions but also (queer as this must sound) in judgments. This seems to abolish logic, but does not do so – It is one thing to describe methods of measurement, and another to obtain and state results of measurement. But what we call 'measuring' is partly determined by a certain constancy in results of measurement.
>
> (Wittgenstein 1984:88)

Agreement in the meaning of words, in the meaning of what we say to one another, leads us towards the view that knowledge is social, that our understanding of the world that we communicate to others is subject to a process of interpersonal interpretation. The value of the science language game or the logic language game is that words are used only after considerable care has been given to their definition. None the less, misinterpretation and misleading use can occur. The safeguard is still to be found in the negotiation of meaning.

Although we place much of the onus on the transmitter of information, the receiver certainly bears some of the responsibility for the quality of communication. In counselling, it is an established practice to reflect back to the client what the client has been saying:

'Let me just see if I've got it clear what you've been telling me'

or

'So what you're saying is ...'

The counsellor, in stating her interpretation of the picture so far, is checking that this interpretation is in line with what the client intended. A similar responsibility belongs to all of us receiving a message, especially when the message is ambiguous, conveys emotions, or causes emotions. It is in these circumstances that we are likely to stay silent or to give the message an interpretation that might not have been what the speaker intended. Each of us can produce a running commentary in our heads of the conversation that we are having. The commentary is an interaction at a thought level between what we hear and our own system for making sense of the world, which includes that conversation. Too often, we interpret silently and misinterpret. We get the other person wrong. The only way of preventing that is to seek clarification and to check out whether our interpretation is correct. These are difficult inter-personal skills. They are the basis for good communication, for good interpersonal relationships, and for team work. They may be crucial skills for young people to acquire and this causes us to consider how they can develop such skills.

The relevance of this view to educational practice shows itself in a number of ways. At one level, it provides a very important reason for teaching interpersonal skills. If people learn to regard meaning as something which cannot be taken for granted but which must be negotiated, then the quality of their interactions will be enhanced. At another level, such a view provides a rationale for the teacher in pursuing a questioning attitude towards the way language is used in text-books, in academic reference books, in policy documents, in their own lesson notes, hand-outs, and letters to parents. Adopting a more wary approach to language, how one uses it oneself, and how it is used by others, is a vital part of education for young people and forms one part of the approach that Postman and Weingartner (1969) call 'crap-detecting'.

The safeguarding of our political and intellectual freedoms may require teachers to show the next generation of students how to analyse language carefully in order to establish what is being communicated. At the very least, people need to feel a sense of unease with arguments that are too slick, and with communications that are heavily loaded so as to appeal to one's emotions rather than to one's reason. Spotting propaganda is a useful skill, but it might be also that out-and-out propaganda is easier to spot than the choice of certain metaphors, the employment of certain terms, and the reference to particular authority figures, as means of influence.

Part III

Part III addresses some of the psychological factors that shape the lives, behaviour, and career choices of teachers. We start by examining the role of psychology in education and the way this is usually introduced to teachers. We look at the work of psychologists who argue that many of these influential factors operate without our being aware of their impact on our relationships with colleagues and children. We discuss the role of early upbringing and family life on teachers and consider the impact of these on classroom practice. We conclude Part III by highlighting what we see to be key areas to be acknowledged, if we seek to engage in straight and open communication.

Part III is written in a different style to the rest of the book. So far we have debated a range of issues and asked you to examine the way values, myths, and language influence educational practice. In Part III we describe, rather than debate, the psychological perspectives we introduce. You are in the best position to relate these views to your own life and relationships with others, and to determine how valid they are for you.

Chapter Eight

Perspectives on teachers and children

After looking at how individual values and beliefs emerge in the educational debate and considering the implications of language usage, it is now necessary to take a closer look at teachers themselves and their own life histories, as an important factor in determining how they teach. There are few other professional groups whose role and worth is debated so frequently in the media, and of whom the public at large have themselves such extensive first-hand experience.

We have suggested that many messages are conveyed to teachers, both overtly and, perhaps more significantly, covertly, from the beginning of their professional lives as students and then throughout their careers as teachers. We do not feel it would be appropriate for us to encourage teachers to look closely and examine the underlying motivation and messages of others if they did not also look critically at their own attitudes and values and consider the impact of these on their educational practice. Our exhortations for teachers to question others with whom they have contact within the education system would have a hollow ring to it if we did not attempt this task.

We, therefore, wish to go a little further in pursuing this theme by also looking at how the influences of childhood, and life with our parents or guardians, have a profound impact on the people we are today. They affect how we see the world, how we develop as people, and the nature of our interactions with others. Alexander (1984) in the introduction to his book *Primary Teaching* writes: 'Teachers are the product not merely of their training but of their unique intellectual attributes, their personality, attitudes and cumulative experiences. Their own experiences as children (or parents) may profoundly influence their approach to the children they teach' (Alexander 1984:3).

We are not always consciously aware of how previous experiences influence and shape the people we are today. In this chapter we will briefly look at the way psychology has typically been introduced to teachers, assess the likely impact of this, and then consider an alternative to previous trends. We will discuss whether psychology may be of greater value to teachers in the light of insights it can offer into their own behaviour, rather than as a way of attempting to understand children.

We will argue that teachers should examine critically their own roles, motives, behaviour, attitudes, beliefs, and values, and consider such influences on how they teach, as a first step in enhancing classroom practice. In so doing we will again touch on some of the themes raised in Chapter Four in our discussion on psychological influences on the curriculum.

Psychology, teachers, and education

Psychology, together with history, philosophy, and sociology, has been one of the disciplines that education has typically drawn on, as a theoretical basis to inform the teaching process. A psychology element has featured in the training of most teachers and the popularity of books such as Denis Child's *Psychology and the Teacher* (1986 and now in its fourth edition) testifies to this.

Much of the psychology to which teachers, and those intending to teach, have been introduced has been concerned exclusively with children and their development. Educationalists who have drawn upon theories from psychology have attempted to show teachers how children typically develop, so that teachers have some idea of how children might be expected to behave and learn in the classroom. This emphasis has helped create, for teachers and others involved in educating children, notions of what is 'normal development' and what is not normal.

Early educationalists such as Rousseau and Montessori were clearly interested in children's development and the kind of environments that enabled this to flourish. More recently the theories of Piaget have had a substantial influence on educational thinking and practice. In Chapter Three we examined the impact of developmental psychology in the three areas of: curriculum content, teaching style, and assessment and curriculum evaluation.

We also identified what we see to be a negative influence of this psychology on teaching children, namely that when a child experiences either learning or behavioural difficulties, something is seen to be 'wrong' with the child, rather than with any aspect of the child's learning environment. However, this is rarely considered by advocates of a developmental approach, when discussing its educational implications. The quality of relationships and the overall nature of the classroom environment is recognized as being of considerable importance but is rarely identified as a potential cause of a child's difficulties. This is much more likely to be attributed to a child's level of social, emotional, and intellectual development.

Yet we know from our own experiences of school as pupils, how important the learning environment created by a teacher was in facilitating progress. We probably tended to be interested in those subjects taught by teachers we preferred. Similarly we are likely to have been less positively disposed towards those subjects where we had more difficulty in relating to the teacher. We can therefore speculate that a key factor, in determining whether or not a child is going to experience difficulties, is subject content and the quality of pupil–teacher relationships.

Alexander comments briefly on applications of psychology to teaching:

> An examination of student texts and course syllabuses will reveal that most deal not so much with the psychology of *education* as with the psychology of the *child*, and that child's education is treated only in so far as it can be conceived independently of the person who is its chief architect, the teacher.
>
> (Alexander 1984:93)

Alexander develops this theme and regrets that popular textbooks about psychology for teachers (Child 1981 edition, and Fontana 1981) concentrate almost exclusively on the learner.

What is interesting is that this view is supported more recently by Child in an article reviewing the history of educational psychology. He comments:

> Variation in the performance of children was placed squarely on their shoulders. Poor performance was put down to lack of effort or lack of ability on their part. What about the teachers? The fact is that the teacher's role, both in terms of personal qualities *and* details of the task of teaching, was almost ignored up to the 1950s. As editor of the British Journal of Educational Psychology, I commissioned a cumulative index from 1930 to 1980. It's a most instructive document on the changing interests in the subject over that period. Entries relating to teachers occurred six times in the first twenty-five years (1930–54) and twenty-seven times in the last twenty-five years (1955–80).
>
> (Child 1985:13–14)

Child doubts whether the areas that have provided the focus of this work – teacher personality, affective style, or attitudes to authority and misbehaviour – can be altered. He believes they are 'pretty well impervious to change' (p. 15). This is an area we examine in later chapters in Part III but at this point what needs to be said is that it is not just a question of whether teachers cannot change, but whether they *know* they cannot change and that the aforementioned areas may be contributory factors influencing children's classroom behaviour. However, Child proposes that there is much that teachers can change in the classroom in relation to learning and teaching and this is very much reflected in his book *Applications of Psychology for the Teacher* (1986).

Rarely therefore, until fairly recently, have attempts been made to look at the relevance of psychology to the nature of classroom interactions that take place each day. Books such as Bull and Solity (1987), and Robertson (1981) begin to do this in relation to the management of children's behaviour. The area of psychology on which they frequently draw is behavioural psychology, which itself has been the subject of much criticism (See Chapter Four).

Nevertheless, what these texts advocate is that teachers begin to examine their own behaviour in the classroom as a starting point for positive classroom interactions. To assert this position is not to ignore the importance of the child, and an understanding of the world of children, but to acknowledge that teachers make a significant difference to the nature of classroom interactions. Similarly, Bull and Solity suggest that when teachers experience difficulties in managing the behaviour of a child, the starting point for beginning to resolve this is for the teacher to begin to ask some pertinent questions about *why* a particular child is felt to be a problem. A teacher's assertion that a child is experiencing difficulties cannot be divorced from a detailed look at *what* the problem is and *why* it is a problem for that particular teacher.

Many of the child-centred critics (see Chapter Four) of behavioural psychology have argued that it aims to 'modify' children's behaviour through the systematic use of rewards, that it pays little attention to the interests and desires of the children themselves, and does not encourage pupil autonomy and responsibility. Since the emphasis of these writers is on the child, they have naturally looked at behavioural psychology from a child-centred perspective and interpreted it in terms of what they perceive teachers do to children. As a result they have neglected the emphasis of other writers who do not see behavioural psychology as a means of changing pupils, but as providing a framework within which teachers can monitor and evaluate *their own behaviour*. The account of behavioural psychology in Bull and Solity is very much teacher orientated and looks at the overall classroom environment, the nature of relationships between pupils and teachers, and how children can be helped to become responsible for their own behaviour. It is incumbent on teachers to take responsibility for offering children appropriate experiences. What children learn or how they develop will to some extent be directly related to the quality of those experiences.

The positive side of this is that teachers can take a share of the credit when children make satisfactory progress; the negative side is that it is their responsibility if they fail to do so. Children cannot be made the scapegoat for a lack of progress. Clearly not everyone will find it comfortable to adopt this position, which is certainly more personally threatening than claiming the child has a difficulty.

One particular implication of this is that what teachers say about children has to be considered in the light of what it also implies about the teacher. This point has also been made by Postman and Weingartner (1969) who believe that any statement a teacher makes about a child is initially and indirectly revealing something about that teacher, rather than informing us about the pupil:

> For example, we say 'John is stupid' or 'Helen is smart' as if 'stupidity' and 'smartness' were characteristics of John and Helen. A literal translation of 'John is stupid' (that is its most scientific meaning) might go something like this: 'When I perceive John's behaviour, I am disappointed or distressed or frustrated or disgusted. The sentence I use to express my perceptions and evaluations of these events is 'John is stupid'.
>
> (Postman and Weingartner 1969:101–12)

The shift in emphasis from child to teacher is most readily seen in books about the management of children's behaviour. However, other writers are also beginning to make increased reference to an under-standing of teachers and their backgrounds as an important feature in understanding the educative process. So, for example, Nias (1989) examines the needs of a group of teachers who comprised subjects for her longitudinal study of early and mid-career teachers in primary and middle schools. She has looked at their personal investment in their jobs and offered comments on this from a psychological and sociological perspective.

There is also a small but increasing literature on teachers and their careers (Ball and Goodson 1985; Sikes *et al.* 1985). This looks at some of the personal factors that affect teachers' perceptions of how they carry out their role within a largely sociological framework. Despite these examples, much of what is written in the area of psychology in education tends to be about the psychology of children, although, as we have suggested, this imbalance is in the process of being redressed to some extent.

Family influences

So why might it be important for teachers to become aware of the issues that are important to them and of aspects of their own personality that might have a direct bearing on how they interpret events and behave in the classroom? The preoccupation with child development and the concept of matching the curriculum to a child's 'stage' of development

113

arose from the belief that understanding and knowledge about the child would give teachers insights and a platform from which to interact and engage children in varied, meaningful, and valid learning experiences. However, the question this raises is whether it is possible to achieve an understanding and appreciation of a child's behaviour and development without also having some kind of insights into your own behaviour? What are we to make of the teacher who in Postman and Weingartner's example refers to a child as being 'smart' or 'thick' but has no appreciation of the personal disclosure evident in such a statement? Is the emphasis on child psychology to the exclusion of adult psychology misplaced?

We are not suggesting that teachers' individual statements and observations about children need to be accompanied by a declaration of personal awareness; this would clearly be untenable. We are also not suggesting that a kind of 'therapeutic police force' check out the suitability of those engaged in teaching children to ensure that they don't have any skeletons in the cupboard. Nor are we recommending that teachers go into 'therapy' to confront suppressed childhood memories. Rather, what we are advocating is that teachers first of all recognize the importance of their own backgrounds as key factors in how they look at children, teaching, and events in the classroom; that how they were treated as children may well have a bearing on the way in which they too, in turn, relate to children in their care; and that there will be echoes of their own upbringing in the way they face the tasks and challenges of teaching.

In this context, it is often a source of puzzlement to those outside the field of psychotherapy, that therapists themselves have to undergo a period of analysis before becoming fully qualified therapists. Furthermore, for many therapists this is something they choose to do well beyond their initial training. One reason for this is the recognition that it is not deemed possible to work constructively with others in a therapeutic context without considerable personal awareness.

Although the roles of teacher and therapist are not the same, there are some areas of overlap. Both groups are often attempting to facilitate the development of either children or clients. This is often done by helping the target group to learn for themselves, through reflecting on their own experiences. Clearly during such interactions there are crisis points, and it is perhaps at these times when the teacher or therapist needs to be aware of the issues that affect them most deeply (Measor 1985, Wheldall and Merrett 1988).

Increasingly, as teachers embark on projects designed to facilitate children's personal and social development (Lang 1988), it is becoming even more important that they take the opportunity to reflect on the impact of their own backgrounds. It is interesting to note that in the book edited by Lang (which offers a wide range of perspectives and approaches to personal and social education in primary schools), there are few references to teachers engaging in this type of endeavour. The impression created is that personal and social education is something teachers provide for children without it requiring that teachers reflect on their past and the issues they find uncomfortable, which may have a bearing on their teaching.

Much then that has happened in applying psychology to education has reflected the view that psychology is a body of knowledge that teachers can use to help them understand children. It has not been viewed reflectively and been seen that it could also shed light on the broader context of daily classroom interactions, or provide teachers with frameworks for reflecting on their own personal histories and their impact on their role as teachers.

Let us now turn to why psychology has rarely been presented to those intending to teach as a platform for self-appraisal and self-reflection. Perhaps one reason is that to do so might feel threatening, both to lecturers and students on initial teacher education courses, and invariably we put a lot of energy into avoiding threatening and uncomfortable feelings and emotions.

Most readers of this book, as well as having come across Piaget, are likely to have heard of Sigmund Freud. He was one of the first psychologists to investigate the significance of early childhood on the development of personality. Whilst much of what he said is still the subject of heated debate, he articulated a number of concepts to explain how individuals attempt to defend their images of themselves from attack. Concepts such as displacement, repression, projection, and sublimation were all offered as explanations of how individuals would attempt to protect their own 'ego'. The handy person round the house who blames his or her tools when things don't work out as planned may also be the teacher who blames the children for failing to behave appropriately. Why are these positions adopted? Usually as a form of defence, reflecting an unwillingness to acknowledge things about ourselves that we find unpleasant or uncomfortable.

Accepting responsibility

It is this concentration on child rather than adult psychology in teacher education which motivates us to take a look at how theories drawn from the fields of counselling and interpersonal psychology may be applied reflectively. We start from the premise that self-awareness is a necessary starting point for encouraging and facilitating the development of others.

The theories we present in Chapters Nine and Ten have much in common. In particular they highlight that we are not always aware of exactly what leads us to behave as we do, especially in our personal and professional relationships with others. They stress the importance of earlier life experiences in shaping these interactions and emphasize the role our parents play in this process. The perspectives we offer are intended to help individuals reflect upon their own behaviour and the factors that might promote it, as a means of establishing more positive relationships in the future.

In addition, the theories embody three important principles that we would support. First, in the words of Eric Berne (1964), everyone is born 'OK'. Berne had a positive view of human nature which he stated in the phrase 'I am OK; you are OK'. He believed that people's less desirable characteristics represented patterns of behaviour which become a way of coping with negative family influences. Steiner explains this position as follows: 'people have a natural tendency to live, to take care of themselves, to be happy, to learn to get along with each other, and to respect other forms of life' (Steiner 1974:4). Everyone is seen to have the capacity for leading independent, fulfilling lives and to engage in rewarding relationships with others. Hence the view that everyone starts out life 'OK'. It is invariably the influence of our upbringing that diverts us from this course and leads us to be 'not OK'.

The second principle is that no one is to blame for this happening. The fact that we develop less than positive ways of interacting is nobody's fault. We might like to think that it is and actively lay the blame at someone else's door. The theories we discuss encourage us to accept *responsibility for our own behaviour*.

The third principle is that we can change those aspects of our behaviour that we dislike and that make us feel uncomfortable. However, whether this happens is down to us rather than anyone else. We cannot request that others change, only how we choose to interact with them.

It may appear in what has been said so far, and what follows, that parents are coming in for a lot of criticism and that they are seen as the causes of everything that goes wrong with their offspring, both as children and later as adults. Parents quite patently and undeniably have a profound influence on their children. Yet it would not be right to hold them responsible for the ills of their children. The point is explained by Robin Skynner, the well-known psychiatrist and family therapist, and John Cleese, the actor and comedian, in the popular, and widely read book *Families and How to Survive Them* (1984). They state that parents behave as they do in relation to their children because that is how they were treated by their own parents. And their parents behaved as they did because of their own parents. In other words, patterns of behaviour are established within families and get handed down from one generation to the next, in much the same way as the best china and family memor-abilia. Parents therefore are not so much to blame, as part of a very sophisticated pattern of events.

The psychological theories we discuss in the following chapters represent a departure from how psychology is typically presented to the teaching profession. We are sceptical about delving too deeply into the personal lives of pupils, especially when those doing so are reluctant to examine their own backgrounds and life histories. Furthermore, we have only to think how long it would take an outsider to get a full under-standing of the complex nature of our own family dynamics, to appreciate how difficult it might be to get comparable insights into a child's background.

The areas of psychology we present, therefore, offer a framework which enables teachers to reflect on their own roles, attitudes, values, and behaviour, as a way of understanding their contribution to the teaching and learning processes. We start in the next chapter by examining the theories of George Kelly, and in particular his theory of personal constructs, which offers insight into how teachers might begin to perceive the classroom environment.

Chapter Nine

The personal world of teachers

It may seem strange that in a book in which we have chosen to question some established assumptions about the nature of science, we are drawn to the theories of a psychologist, George Kelly, who once famously asserted that 'all men are scientists'. However, as we shall see, he was referring to the way in which people proceeded to make sense of their personal worlds rather than how they pursued 'scientific truths'.

Kelly developed the theory of personal construct psychology. It rarely featured in psychology text books written in the 1960s and early 1970s but has recently attracted increasing attention within the world of education, as well as psychology. For example, Salmon (1988) has devoted an entire book to a description and discussion of the relevance of personal construct psychology to teachers. Similarly, it is now appearing in some general educational textbooks for teachers (e.g. Pollard and Tann 1987), where its value is related briefly to teacher investigations into children's perceptions of classrooms.

Kelly, in his work as a psychologist, wished to see 'clients' as equals. He eschewed the notion that he, as a therapist, was in any way superior to the clients with whom he came into contact. He also did not regard himself to be the possessor of 'greater knowledge' which would enable him to explain their problems. Rather he perceived that people interpret the world and construe events going on around them in, for them, entirely reasonable and valid ways. He did not wish to impose his own view of the world on others. Instead, his preferred role as a psychologist was to help clients make sense of their lives through coming to understand how they interpreted events, by using their own frames of reference to explain personal experiences, so they would understand their own world a little better. This was, however, a less than familiar position to take in the world of psychology at a time when psychologists typically viewed themselves as having specialized knowledge and theories which could be applied to the lives of their clients. In this way psychologists, as possessors of knowledge, had a certain amount of power over those they were seeking to help.

Kelly maintained that each of us has our own unique view of the world which is influenced by our families and experiences in life. The sense we might make of our lives is seen as a reasonable response to our personal experiences and more valid than any interpretation offered by an 'expert psychologist'. The psychology of personal constructs is a theory which tries to unlock those personal life histories and explain how they shape our behaviour and perceptions of others.

Within a Kellian view of the world, it is assumed that an individual's perceptions of life are understandable and legitimate in terms of earlier experiences. We might not like or agree with how others view life, but we cannot readily deny or invalidate their perceptions. Inevitably such a view has significant implications for how certain types of interactions are interpreted in the classroom by teachers, especially when they are unwelcome or of a disruptive nature.

'Man as a scientist'

So what did Kelly mean when he asserted that people proceeded in life as if they were scientists? Kelly saw parallels between how individuals tried to make sense of the world and how scientists conducted themselves during their experiments. Scientists adopt certain procedures when investigating various phenomena. They start with a hypothesis which incorporates a prediction about what might happen in the world when certain conditions prevail. A scientist might hypothesize about the physical and chemical properties of the environment and then set up a series of experiments to test out the hypothesis under carefully controlled conditions. Further experiments might then be required to assess the overall generalizability of the findings.

Kelly proposed that the way individuals make sense of their own environments is very similar to that of the scientist. Through their observations and experience of life, hypotheses are formulated about what is going on around them. They generate predictions about this world and then begin to test out their hypotheses. Just as a scientist records and evaluates the results of his experiments, so does 'the hypothesis testing' person. What any individual predicts will happen in the future is related to what actually happened in the past. These outcomes form the basis of predictions about, and interactions with, others.

The sense we make of people is linked to some extent to our capacity to predict outcomes within a social context. Inevitably this can be related to our families and early childhood experiences. It is interesting to note how Penelope Leach discusses children's interpretations of the world in her widely read handbook on parenting and raising children (Leach 1979). When discussing the first year of a child's life, she asks parents to reflect on what their children will learn from how they behave

119

as parents. She suggests that children's understanding of the world is heavily influenced by interactions with their parents. Leach stresses the significance of establishing appropriate patterns of behaviour early in a child's experiences so they can begin to make sense of life.

Young children are constantly engaged in the process of hypothesis testing in their attempts to understand their surroundings. The clearer patterns of behaviour appear, the more likely children are to appreciate the significance of what is happening and to recognize that much of our behaviour is governed by subtle, but well-established, social rules and rituals. If all families were to abide by the same rules and construed life in exactly the same ways, we would find it considerably easier to appreciate the perceptions of any particular child. However, this does not happen, and for teachers it is important to recognize each child's unique understanding of the world.

The hypothesis testing that takes place is initially restricted to the child's immediate home environment and it usually, therefore, takes some time before the child, as a 'home-based' scientist, has to apply her knowledge of the world to wider and more varied social settings. In fact, for many children, school will be one of their first experiences of an extended world, since their main contact outside the immediate family network is still within fairly safe and familiar social settings, perhaps extended family contact or visits to friends and their families.

When children begin school they are entering a whole new world. It is quite staggering sometimes to stand back and look at how much they have learned before their first encounters with formal education. They have mastered a comprehensive range of physical skills, such as walking, running, and jumping. They have learned to talk (and in so doing have mastered many complex linguistic skills) and they are sophisticated social beings. They have acquired a range of subtle social skills which, when the occasion arises, they can apply with considerable sophistication and even ruthlessness.

Much early learning helps children to establish the permanence of physical features in life. Objects around the house retain their identity irrespective of changes that are made to them. A chair is always a chair whether it be upright or lying on the floor. So is a table or a cup or a knife or any other objects with which they have previously had contact. The demands of school offer many children a sharp contrast to life as they have previously known it. They become engaged in a series of personal 'experiments', to see how far their existing perceptions serve them in their new environment. The degree of stability they have come to expect changes as they learn to read and write. Meaning is conveyed through position as well as shape. For example the numeral '3' can also be the letter 'm' or the letter 'w'. The significance of the symbol '3' varies depending on its position, and so challenges children's previous assumptions.

Similarly, the patterns of behaviour which were acceptable at home may not be accepted at school. Movement around the classroom is sometimes restricted. They cannot eat just when they like. They can only go outside with the prior approval of the teacher. Instead of having either the sole attention of one adult, or sharing that adult with three or four children, a child has to compete with twenty or thirty others for the teacher's time. Life is less predictable and less certain for the child than it was. Previous constructions of the world have to be put to the test and may need revising. Think how we, as adults, respond to a new job or changes in our personal circumstance. We are likely to experience some degree of stress when we are required to make changes in our lives. Change implies that the assumptions on which our daily schedules and routines are based may be challenged and may need to be re-examined. Imagine then the demands being made on a four- or five-year-old, as she proceeds in her new world.

This process of hypothesis testing is not restricted to the early years of life. According to Kelly, it is something we do throughout our lives, although the extent to which we need to reinterpret life is invariably determined by the number of new situations we encounter. When our daily lives follow familiar and accepted patterns there is naturally less need to constantly revise our existing hypotheses. We have already formed clear perceptions of the world and our place in it. Within certain limits we are able to make those necessary predictions about our daily interactions and relationships with others for life to have some stability and coherence.

Making sense of the world

The argument so far then, is that the experiments that scientists conduct give us information about the world. So it is with our personal experiments and 'scientific pursuits'. We reflect on our observations and begin to arrive at a picture of the world that helps us make sense of what we see going on around us. The construction we place on events invariably differs from that of others but is no less valid for that.

Kelly offered a conceptual framework through which sense could be made of various perceptions held by different people. He suggested that we view the world through what he called 'constructs'. They are a kind of template through which we observe life and can be thought of as series of continua which incorporate and reflect our most important attitudes and values. In a moment we shall explain what we mean by 'continua'.

First of all let us illustrate how we use our personal constructs. Imagine you have been to a party and are trying to describe someone you met there to a friend. You might say that the person was attractive, intelligent, happy, sensitive, humorous, or thoughtful. This is the way any of us might describe the characteristics of another. We draw attention to specific attributes that we notice and which seem important to us. In this example the qualities identified would generally be seen as desirable and positive. An alternative description might have identified less positive traits, such as boring, self-centred, ruthless, thoughtless, or insensitive.

The first thing to note is that however we describe someone, whether it be in positive or negative terms or a combination of the two, we notice the things that matter to us most. Our descriptions, as well as conveying something of the other person, also say something about ourselves. We are revealing information about the criteria we apply to our observations of others.

Second, our descriptions are not entirely complete. In describing someone as attractive, intelligent, sensitive, or humorous, we were only giving half the story. Kelly felt it was only possible to understand the meaning of someone else's constructs when you knew the opposite of these terms. For one individual the opposite of attractive might be unattractive. For someone else it might be poorly dressed. Similarly the opposite of intelligent for some might be unintelligent, but for others lazy. It could also be argued that there may well be considerable differences in the perceptions of two people, where for one the opposite of happy is sad, but for another it is suicidal.

The descriptions offered earlier can be more fully appreciated when the opposites are also given. It is through these continua or bi-polar statements, which Kelly referred to as constructs, that he believes we interpret the world.

Salmon (1988) explores a range of factors that influence the sense children make of the world of school and teachers. She suggests that this is based, to some extent, on the prior knowledge children have about the nature of schools and their purpose. Salmon refers to research which looks at the social and cultural backgrounds of teachers in relation to those of children. As might be expected, the understanding that children have of school and life in the classroom is influenced by the match between their social and cultural origins and those of their teachers. It clearly cannot be assumed that children share a teacher's perceptions of events in school. There will be overlap between the two but it is also likely that certain events and aspects of life in the classroom will be seen differently by teachers and pupils.

In earlier chapters we introduced a number of 'educational constructs' about the curriculum and teaching: progressive and traditional;

child-centred and teacher-directed; behavioural and developmental; and objectives (what is learned) and process (how it is learned). They can also be seen as representing the differing construct systems of the authors we quote. What is apparent is that there are not universally agreed understandings of what any of these terms mean. They are open to a range of interpretations.

The sense a developmentalist has of behavioural psychology is very different to that of the behaviourist. Similarly, the 'objectives–process' construct has different meanings for the adherents of different theoretical perspectives. The developmental approach is usually seen to be all about 'the process' rather than learning outcomes. However, we offered another interpretation of these terms in Chapter Four, from a behavioural perspective, which disputes that either developmental or behavioural approaches are exclusively all about outcomes or all about the process.

Educational debate reflects individual constructs which incorporate values and beliefs. We believe that appreciating this creates a different agenda for the spectator on the touchline of the 'education game'. The way forward is not only about getting better data or presenting better arguments but also about ascertaining the constructs of the various participants in such a dialogue and beginning to understand how they view the world and each other.

The possibility of alternative constructions

The clear implication of what we have said so far is that resolving differing perceptions is not a simple matter of saying one is right and the other wrong. It involves employing a key tenet of personal construct psychology, enshrined in what is known as the principle of constructive alternativism. This states that all events are open to more than one interpretation. There may not be correct and incorrect perceptions, only different ones. This principle acknowledges that the world can be construed in many ways, that our constructions are not the only ones that are possible. We may see events one way, but the interpretations of others are not only possible but equally valid to our own.

If teachers in schools recognize the implications of constructive alternativism, we suspect that their understanding of events in the school day will be enriched. When events run smoothly and are in accordance with the wishes of the teacher, differences in perceptions between teachers and pupils are not always apparent and, if they are, rarely cause concern, as they can be comfortably tolerated by the teacher, and may even give rise to lively discussion and debate. However, where a child is seen to misbehave, the invariably distinct and different perceptions of teacher and child have to be reconciled. It is on such occasions that teachers may find it difficult to acknowledge the perceptions of the child as legitimate.

If we accept that there are alternative constructions to everyday classroom events, it might be helpful to examine a typical clash of constructs between teacher and pupil. We take as our example the conflict of interest which invariably underlies the labelling of a child as 'disruptive' by a teacher. To experience the effects of a disruptive pupil is clearly uncomfortable and threatening. At such times it is also understandable that a teacher is not necessarily well disposed to speculating on how the child might be seeing matters. But let us stop for a moment and look at events from the child's point of view.

First of all, it can be argued that to be an effective 'disruptive pupil' is to engage in highly skilled social behaviour. A child would have to be able to anticipate the teacher's behaviour in response to certain circumstances. In many instances the child also needs to be able to predict how other children will respond to their misbehaviour. There has to be some pay-off for being disruptive and this might arise from the teacher's and pupils' reactions to what is done. A failure to predict this may well leave the disruptive act having entirely different and less satisfactory consequences for the pupil concerned.

A teacher who is open to the possibility that events can be reinterpreted and reconstrued will, in our view, be a different 'kind of teacher' to someone who cannot. To acknowledge that children have a point of view is to open up the potential for negotiation and to recognize the legitimacy of children's perceptions. It is to see them in some sense as equals, as people with rights to hold valid observations of, and reactions to, classroom life.

The same can be said of educational theorists who adopt adversarial positions. The tendency towards confrontation hides, if it ever existed, any desire to explore a negotiated resolution of differing perspectives. We would see that such a course of action might enhance classroom practice and, to the extent that the principle of negotiation is applied in the classroom, would certainly present children with different models of how adults resolve differences. We wonder whether the teacher who is wedded to any particular view of the world, to the exclusion of all others, will be in a position to acknowledge the perceptions children have of school life.

The teacher's constructs

Within a Kellian framework, a teacher's descriptions of a child, whether positive (i.e., industrious, thoughtful, caring, creative) or negative (i.e., disruptive, disobedient, aggressive, uninterested in work) may or may not be revealing something about the child. What they are unmistakably doing, is highlighting aspects of the teacher's own construct system and reaction to the child in question. Such descriptors reveal something of the personal world of the teacher and the teacher's perceptions of a child and of classroom events. It is the teacher we learn about, not necessarily the child.

It is possible to rephrase and reconstrue the teacher's observations of the 'disruptive child'. Perhaps what the teacher is saying is: 'I find this pupil's behaviour to be disruptive in my lessons. He does not carry out my instructions and I find his presence personally threatening. He is not interested in the work I provide'. In all probability the pupil also has another version of events which would be equally valid. In personal construct psychology the pupil has a point of view and perceptions of events which can contribute more fully to our appreciation of classroom interactions.

To see children in this way runs counter to the way adults often view children. Just as in many areas of therapeutic psychology, the psychologist is cast in the role of expert who exerts power over his clients, so it often is in the classroom. Teachers are in positions where they similarly exercise power over their pupils. It may be, however, that it is only when things go wrong during a lesson or activity that we get a more accurate perception of classroom life. It is when events do not proceed in the desired manner that teachers are likely to be feeling under stress and this makes it increasingly difficult to maintain a desired professional persona.

Being angry or frustrated can often have the effect of leading people to behave in ways which are consistent with how they feel. This may prompt a teacher to say what they really think about a child, even though they may regret having done so at some point in the future. This phenomenon is not only evidenced in the classroom, it happens within family settings as well. When parents and children are feeling under stress or threatened, they are much more likely to 'let off steam' and say what they really think and feel, revealing more of their construct system and firmly held perceptions.

Our work as educational psychologists has made us familiar with scenarios of this type in schools. When invited into schools to talk about children who are presenting problems, it is often the case that judgements have already been made about the child in the light of their behaviour. It is as if a teacher's status gives him this right. We have rarely encountered situations where, after being given a teacher's perceptions of events, that teacher has provided his observations of how the pupil might be construing matters.

It may appear that we are being unduly harsh on teachers here. This is not our intention and, to be fair, there have been occasions when we have colluded with the view that the 'problem' is the child, not the child's learning environment. Our concern at the moment is to highlight an implication of Kellian psychology which emphasizes that the perceptions of pupils are as relevant as those of teachers. Furthermore, pupils' perceptions need to be acknowledged and considered in any real attempt to understand events in the classroom. In our experience the very act of allowing children to offer their perceptions, particularly for discussion with teachers, can often have positive outcomes for all concerned.

Pupils are in a similarly vulnerable position when it is claimed by teachers or parents that they are experiencing a difficulty in learning. Solity (1988) and Solity and Bull (1987) have offered possible reconstructions of such observations. Inevitably when children fail to make acceptable progress there is an implied threat to a teacher's view of her professional competence. A commonly held perception under these circumstances is that as all the other children have made acceptable progress, the one or two who do not have failed because of a learning difficulty. This explanation is likely to find favour because one alternative would suggest that the children have not been taught adequately.

The perceptions held by the teacher reflect her belief that a failure to learn reflects a lack of ability. If, however, the teacher starts from a different position, an alternative conclusion emerges. If it is assumed that all children can learn, and furthermore can learn in a manner which we find acceptable, however we may wish to define this, then a failure to make progress is the result of a failure on the part of the teacher, so far, to provide an appropriate learning environment.

To continue this reinterpretation, we could speculate that the teacher who starts from this position may, at the end of the school day, call together the children whose progress is causing concern and tell them not to worry, there is clearly something wrong with the way she is teaching. The teacher confides that at the moment she is not sure where the difficulty lies. Such a teacher might ask the children for their observations and opinions about her effectiveness as a teacher. The teacher tells the children that she will go home and give the situation some thought and will see how things go tomorrow. However, our teacher wishes to reassure the children that it is not their problem. They should go home and have a relaxing evening. The teacher knows that they do not have a difficulty, that it is the teacher's problem and that she will get it right soon.

A third interpretation is that the learning process is a conjunction of what the learner brings to the situation as well as the teacher. This recognizes that the child is *also* an active 'sense-maker' of the classroom environment. Within this scenario the teacher and child will jointly seek to resolve the problem. The teacher will invite the child to explain how he sees the problem and what sense he is making of the task.

The teacher in our reconstructions has different perceptions to the one who might suggest that a failure to learn indicates that a child has a learning difficulty. Our teacher assumes that the child is 'OK' and so assumes that a failure to learn implies a 'problem for the teacher'. Our purpose in drawing attention to these issues is to illustrate that classroom events can always be open to alternative explanations. We might not like them, or approve of them, but they can be articulated and may be legitimate.

The value of teaching

In recognizing that pupils are attempting to make sense of school, it must also be acknowledged that teachers are engaged in a similar pursuit of making their professional lives meaningful. Sikes, Measor, and Woods (1985) suggest that the value teachers attach to their work may vary according to a number of factors, some of which will be related to the stage of their careers. Perhaps one reason for the stances taken by teachers, in relation to disruption and learning difficulties that we have discussed, arises where teachers feel unable to attach significance to their jobs.

It is becoming increasingly clear that many teachers are currently feeling disillusioned about their professional lives. They see that the new legislation is making demands which they feel uncomfortable about or do not wish to fulfil. Teaching in the early 1990s is a very different job to the one that may have been experienced in preceding years. For example, as we discussed in Chapter Three, teachers in primary schools have, in the past, had considerable freedom over the curriculum children have followed. Whilst schools have been urged by HMI and LEA advisers and inspectors to develop coherent policies on curriculum matters that run throughout a school, there has been concern from many quarters that this has not always happened. One response to this has been the imposition of a National Curriculum.

There is an inevitable danger that when changes are imposed from outside on organizations, whether they be schools or not, those changes will not necessarily be implemented effectively. Promoting successful change depends to some extent on the commitment of those required to introduce it. The proposals may make sense and be valued by those suggesting them, but be less well received by those who have to implement the changes. An inevitable consequence is that teachers become alienated from the imposed practice.

Salmon would see that this has serious implications within personal construct psychology. She examines the role of teachers within a

Kellian perspective and relates this to curriculum development. She argues that the sense teachers make of what they have to teach is crucial in considering the impact this will have on children.

Many of the psychological theories which are applied to educational settings emphasize children's development and the differences which exist between children. Teachers are often urged to consider the curriculum from the child's point of view and the relevance this will have for pupils. Personal construct psychology, as well as looking at the personal worlds of children, is also teacher focused, and in relation to the curriculum stresses the meanings that teachers attach to what they teach. Salmon writes: 'Education, in this psychology, is the systematic interface between personal construct systems. This view of formal learning puts as much emphasis on teachers' personal meanings as on those of learners' (Salmon 1988:22).

This position is inextricably linked to Kelly's view of knowledge being essentially provisional. Learning in this context is similar to that discussed by Frank Smith (1978) in his article the 'Politics of Ignorance'. Learning is not so much about finding answers as of being aware of the important questions; it is about being aware of how much you don't know rather than how much you do know. Our personal construct systems reflect our knowledge of the world and it is this knowledge that teachers bring to their teaching and their view of the curriculum.

If you look back on your educational career to date, ask yourself the extent to which your choice of subjects, your preferences and dislikes, have been influenced by specific teachers or lecturers and their enthusiasm for, and appreciation of, their chosen fields of study. We are more likely to teach topics well where we are engaged in the subject matter and can attach personal meaning to our efforts.

Personal constructs as stories

Our personal constructs can be seen to embrace the results of our 'scientific inquiries' into life. They represent the sense we have made of life so far and, as Kelly suggested, our constructs can be seen as embodying our 'theories' about life.

In Chapter Five we suggested that the 'truths' discovered by scientists should be regarded as no more than provisional, and merely as our 'best shot' at trying to explain life. We suggested that one way these truths could be viewed was as 'stories' that people wrote and told in an attempt to make sense of the world. Perhaps our constructs should be viewed in a similar way and serve the same purpose for us, in our personal lives, as scientific truths do for the scientist.

Our constructs can, therefore, be seen as our personal stories. They incorporate our theories about what we think is and is not taking place around us in life. However, just as scientists are continually reviewing their theories and interpretations of experimental findings, so we need to do the same with our stories. They provide us with sense and meaning today, but may be revised and updated in the future. As a result, our understanding and knowledge about the world should be viewed as *provisional*. Salmon (1988) presents this position as follows:

> In learning we cannot ever achieve final answers; rather we find new questions, we discover other possibilities we might try out. Knowledge is ultimately governed by constructive alternativism; everything can always be reconstrued.... The understanding that teachers offer is essentially provisional – for the time being. And, for all that school knowledge has high social consensus and is grounded in the whole cultural heritage, it is necessarily personal. It has significance within the personal construct system of the particular teacher. Since each teacher inhabits a distinctive world of meaning, the curriculum of education is constructed afresh, and individually, by every teacher who offers it.
>
> (Salmon 1988:22–3)

Constructs reflect our lives to date, but as our experiments continue throughout life, so our constructs may change in the light of new experiences. Thus Kelly, in drawing parallels between how individuals make sense of life and 'man the scientist', makes an important contribution to the debate about the nature of knowledge discussed in earlier chapters.

In asking us to accept that our personal perceptions of the world may not be shared by anyone else and can, therefore, be open to alternative constructions, personal construct psychology highlights the need to share and negotiate our understanding of the world with others. This coincides with Schutz's views discussed earlier (p. 69).

Theories as personal stories

In Chapter Three, we spent some time discussing the areas in which different elements within the education system try to exert influence over classroom practice. We talked about curriculum content and planning, teaching styles, and assessment and evaluation, and drew attention to some of the theories which underpinned the debate. We would like to suggest that these theories are themselves stories that have been proposed to help explain the world. Piaget and Rousseau, in describing in their differing ways how the development of children could flourish, were revealing their personal accounts, their personal stories of how children learn.

Egan (1983) offers an alternative construction to the developmentalists' position, and rather than seeing that they underpin progressive practice as is often claimed (Blenkin and Kelly 1987), sees such views as potentially hindering children's progress. His arguments and rationale are evidence of an alternative interpretation of the impact of developmental psychology in the classroom. Similarly, we also offered a behavioural interpretation of the classroom which represented different version of events, a different story.

Likewise Postman and Weingartner's (1969) 'story of teaching' offers another perspective on learning based on language usage and questioning. They argue that the purpose of education is to enable students to 'ask questions' and detect the 'hidden' ways their lives are influenced by others. The role of the teacher is to build a curriculum around asking questions, not teaching 'facts'.

What is written about how children learn can be seen as a series of personal stories which are given a certain status because of how they are arrived at, communicated, and presented. These stories, when wrapped up and presented within an academic framework, typically are seen to be more than a personal story. They achieve increased validity and might be seen to represent life as it really is. In so doing, data may not be seen as revealing personal stories, which have to be resolved through negotiation when they conflict. Instead, debates might retreat to increasingly entrenched positions where 'the truth' is defended because it is believed to be based on 'value-free' experimental data.

Much of the controversy we describe in Chapters Three and Four is based on people adopting certain terms as their own, and offering accounts of the teaching and learning process which are 'true', and not open to alternative interpretations. The 'personal stories' of educational theorists are conveyed to intending teachers within the 'education game', in a manner which leads to them becoming accepted representations of 'how things really are'.

In this chapter we have looked at how personal construct psychology can enhance our understanding of classroom life. It encourages personal reflection and a willingness to acknowledge the validity of children's perceptions. In the next chapter we focus our attention on the personal influences on teachers and the impact these have on relationships with both colleagues and children.

Chapter Ten

Understanding teachers

From our discussion so far, the process of negotiation emerges as a key factor in communicating our understanding of the world. Even the findings uncovered by the scientist need to be discussed and debated if they are to gain any general acceptance. Similarly, our personal perceptions are moderated and shaped socially through conversation. This process, whilst enabling differences to be identified and expressed in either scientific findings or personal perceptions, can become problematic. If disagreements are to be resolved, there usually has to be some give-and-take in order that a compromise can be reached. Whether or not divergent perspectives can be reconciled depends on a willingness and ability to negotiate.

Achieving this position is an activity frequently beset by problems. We only have to listen to the news on the television or radio to receive a sharp reminder of how public figures, particularly politicians, stick doggedly to party political loyalties when commenting on issues of general concern. They reaffirm their own positions and 'put down' the opposition, although they may, from time to time, concede some minor point as a debating tactic. They occasionally even create the illusion of negotiating, but this is rarely borne out in reality.

If the views we hold differ from those held by others, a compromise reached through negotiation involves both parties in giving some ground, in letting go of, or modifying, a belief or attitude which might be held very dear. Whether or not we are willing to do this depends on a number of factors, some of which we may not be aware of. This unawareness is not a deliberate attempt to close our eyes to any disconfirmatory or unwelcome information but tends to happen in subtle ways during our lives and is strongly influenced by our early experiences of life.

This chapter speculates on the ways we might question our own behaviour in our professional roles within the education system. Much of what we do in schools may be seen to be governed by patterns of behaviour learned as children, and which are now very much a part of our character but which we may rarely acknowledge. We look behind the scenes and examine the nature of our behaviour and interactions with others.

However, before doing so, we must briefly state that what we suggest in this chapter is somewhat tentative and borne out of our experiences within the education system, rather than being founded on 'scientific evidence' or 'educational research'. Much of the educational literature, as we have said earlier, focuses on children rather than teachers and our aim is to tilt the scales a little in the other direction, towards teachers. In time perhaps our views will influence the 'personal theories' that others hold within educational circles. Our purpose in presenting them here is to enable those currently teaching, or intending to teach, to begin to examine their own behaviour and possible underlying motives for being, or wishing to become, teachers.

We offer some alternative perspectives on the classroom behaviour of teachers and in so doing, draw on those areas of psychology, introduced in Chapter Eight, which can provide teachers with the means to evaluate their own behaviour and motives in the classroom, rather than those of children. We start by asking: why decide to teach?

Why teach?

What are the factors which lead some people to teach but not others? Is it pure chance that some of us are attracted to teaching as a profession whereas many of our contemporaries are not? Doubtless teachers drawing to the end of their careers will look back and reflect on how teaching isn't what it used to be. The educational and political climate in the 1980s and 1990s is very different to the one of previous times. So what might lead a young school-leaver to consider a future as a teacher?

Similarly, for anyone who is already teaching, in those quiet moments when there is space to reflect on life, what are the reasons that spring to mind most readily for choosing such a career? It may be the generous holidays, the fact that you like children, that it's a familiar job, that it's preferable to being in an office, that it's working with people, that there's considerable variety, or that there were no viable alternatives. There may, however, be other factors.

It is sometimes said, but often in a light-hearted way, that you can always spot a teacher outside the classroom. One frequently noted characteristic is a tendency to organize others, whether it be their own families or friends. There is considerable power attached to the role, especially in primary schools, where a single teacher often has total responsibility and control for organizing the daily experiences of perhaps up to thirty or more people.

It is likely that teaching appeals to people with a particular range of personal attributes, just as other professions may appeal to people possessing different characteristics and having different needs. The decision to teach may be determined to some extent by what we perceive our needs to be and how we feel teaching could meet them.

However, is the decision to become a teacher made purely on conscious grounds, or might it be influenced subconsciously, by the environment in which we grew up? The publicly stated reasons for wanting to teach may mask hidden motives that we are less inclined to acknowledge openly. As we suggested earlier, it might be said we choose to teach because we like children and would find the job exciting and challenging. However, teaching also offers opportunities to *control, dominate*, and *organize* others.

Clearly there are a number of influences on our choice of career: education, qualifications, and opportunity. Nevertheless, certain families have a propensity for producing doctors, lawyers, dentists, musicians, or teachers. In a way it is almost as if parents have prepared a 'life plan' which they wish their children to follow. This is a theme we now consider.

Scripts people live

The psychologists Berne (1964) and Steiner (1974) introduced the idea of scripts as a way of understanding some of the choices individuals might make in life. They discuss how parents influence their children, through conveying messages to them about what is, or is not, appropriate behaviour. Often this is along the lines of the well-used aphorism 'do as I say, not as I do'. There are two key elements in this process of parental influence that are known as attributions and injunctions. Attributions tell children what they *can do*, whereas injunctions state what children *must not do*, in order to remain in the parent's favour.

Children are necessarily told what they can and cannot do by their parents. However, the effects of this may be more far-reaching and permanent than we realize. For many of us, parental attributions and injunctions effectively set us on a particular path in life. It is as if a life script has been prepared by parents which they wish their children to follow. Attributions do not go as far as saying, 'teaching is just the job for you', but might in fact be seen to encourage the characteristics required to teach, such as being caring, sensitive, hard-working, and thoughtful. Alternatively, you may have come across people who are consciously striving *not* to meet their parents' expectations, but this could in fact be part of the script. The family dynamics involve parents 'setting up' their children, through giving an overt message to conform, but the covert message is to rebel.

In a sense parents are encouraging their children, through subtle messages, to follow a particular path in life which may even relate to their own ambitions and aspirations. By being seen to comply with parental attributions and injunctions, children relieve the pressure to conform through fulfilling their parents' wishes.

If you reflect on your own reasons for teaching, can any attributions and injunctions be identified that influenced this choice? What factors gave rise to your decision? What other careers were considered? Why were they not pursued? Would they also be considered to be one of the caring professions? Did your parents approve of your choice of career? Would the alternatives have pleased them?

In relation to teacher life scripts, you might like to take a look at Nias (1987, 1989) and Sikes, Measor, and Woods (1985). They have investigated various aspects of teachers' careers, and in what they write it is possible to identify possible life scripts that are being followed by the sample of teachers in their research. We do not discuss these in detail here, since our intention is not to attempt an analysis of teacher life scripts, but to draw attention to their potential influence on our behaviour.

If the decision to become a teacher is related to parental influences which go back some way, might this not affect how an individual fulfils that role? Similarly, might it not contribute to how they interact with colleagues, parents, and children? If successful partnership with parents and collaborative work with colleagues depends on a willingness to negotiate and change our views, how readily will we accept this when our patterns of behaviour have developed over so many years? We invest considerable energy in projecting a desired image of ourselves. How flexible are we really?

Are things as they seem?

If parental factors contribute to our decision to teach, what might affect how we see ourselves in the role of teacher? One major source of influence is, of course, how we see ourselves as people. Our self-image is influenced by others, especially our parents, but, increasingly as we get older, also people outside our family, namely our friends, teachers, partners, or spouses.

Often we try to present what we think are desirable images of ourselves and there may be occasions when we are seen far more positively than we feel is justified. Even when a positive image is ephemeral, the feelings generated are no less real and pleasant while they last. At other times the reverse happens, and the perceptions another person holds about us can be quite negative. This may lead us to experience some discomfort, as we try to resolve these varying perspectives. Why might it be that others do not see us as we wish to be perceived? Why is there a misperception between our real and preferred selves? We believe that considering answers to these questions has a number of implications for teachers.

Furthermore, given that teaching involves continual social interactions with others, whether they be children or colleagues, it is surprising how little time is spent on teacher education courses dealing with this area. To be an effective communicator within educational contexts requires certain levels of personal awareness. When we look beneath the surface of daily interactions in schools, patterns of behaviour can be identified which have considerable implications, but of which the participants may remain unaware.

Imagine a typical school. It's the end of the school day and staff are gradually making their way to the staffroom for a meeting. As they arrive they discuss various aspects of the day in small groups, grabbing cups of tea and coffee en route. What influences choice of friends on the staff? Is it mutual interests, similar philosophies of education, or something else?

Teachers, as they assemble, take part in the continuing discussion. Certain staff appear to take particular stances in relation to the topics being aired. These initial perceptions are reinforced during the course of the staff meeting. One teacher appears critical of every suggestion made by the headteacher whilst another is repeatedly supportive. Another reiterates the principles on which any decision should be made. It appears that what is suggested runs counter to the school philosophy and, furthermore, is not politically acceptable. This teacher offers an idealistic interpretation of school policy. Another attempts to lighten the tone of the debate and makes a joke about everything, thus removing attention from the topic under discussion.

Other roles become apparent, one teacher tries to undermine any decision taken. Although initially appearing to endorse the agreed course of action, he later raises objections, arguing that it will be impossible to implement. A further colleague adopts a defeatist attitude, claiming this has all been tried before and will never work anyway because of external constraints. One member of staff whilst attentive appears passive and does not contribute at all. The person opposite displays a total lack of interest. He leans over to those nearby and whispers comments, he doodles, and at one point appears to be completing his football pools coupon.

Every staffroom is likely to have individuals who occupy some of these roles: passive, critical, undermining, supportive, principled, joker, paranoid, pragmatic, irreverent, disinterested, scapegoat, defeatist, idealist. These individuals may also form various subgroups, like those who have influence over decisions, and those who feel alienated and

135

rarely consulted, if at all, about what happens. Then there are the new members of staff, with ideas for change, and their more established colleagues, who immediately feel wary and resistant to such innovation.

Is this scenario, or a similar one, like a professional social group you have encountered? Studies by Pollard (1987) and Hargreaves (1984) suggest that there is some support for the picture of staffroom life we portray, with Pollard identifying four roles that teachers assume: acceptance, by-passing, subversion, and challenge.

We are suggesting that such patterns of behaviour are learned as children, stay with us throughout life, and possibly represent significant undercurrents to our professional lives. These patterns recur, despite job changes and the varying priorities which emerge as we grow older. Furthermore, they influence our perceptions, and the roles we adopt as teachers in our relationships with colleagues. We may well be aware of some patterns which become established, but perhaps not all of them. Again the significance of this is that it has an adverse effect on our contact with colleagues and prevents us from engaging in an open negotiation, where we are genuinely willing to resolve differences. Let us look at how this might happen.

Looking behind the screen

Skynner and Cleese (1984) discuss how we shield ourselves from our less positive characteristics. They draw on theories from a number of areas and in writing a popular rather than heavily academic book convey, in understandable terms, some of the processes that influence personal development within families. They introduce the analogy of a screen which enables us to separate the bits we like about ourselves from the bits we do not. We display our preferred characteristics, which emerge partly through the attributions and injunctions we receive, in front of the screen and our less acceptable characteristics are placed behind the screen.

Skynner and Cleese suggest that as we grow up, we have the capacity to display the full range of emotions. However, we rarely do so and it is more usual to find that some emotions are more permanent features of our behaviour patterns than others. Which ones feature prominently is determined by our families and their reactions to different emotional states. It is proposed by Skynner and Cleese that whole families generally have the same characteristics placed in front of and behind their screens. So members of a family in which any display of anger is viewed negatively, will attempt to conceal such feelings, as they are unlikely to meet with approval. Whether we find ourselves adopting the position of sceptic, idealist, scapegoat, realist, or pragmatist is related to what is placed in front of, and behind, the screen. Hence discussions in school can be seen to involve not only the specific issues which get aired but social dynamics as well. Thus, being argumentative, accommodating, or considerate may relate more to the personalities of the participants than anything directly attributable to the subject being debated. This, according to Skynner and Cleese, can be traced back to family influences.

There are three implications of our behaviour reflecting what has been placed in front of, or behind, our screen. The first is that we often behave in ways which are the opposite of how we feel. We do this so as not to reveal those traits which were unacceptable within our families as we were growing up and which we learned to cover up.

The second implication is that, in our various social interactions, we are invariably on our 'best behaviour', and attempt to project the image of ourselves that we prefer and that we hope will create a positive impact on others. However, as time passes and we spend more time with people, we find that the side of our behaviour we would prefer to keep out of public view, the areas that might carry a 'user beware' warning, keep emerging. We might not wish it to be known that we are argumentative or aggressive and yet we become aware that these aspects of our behaviour are increasingly evident in our interactions. As we become more uneasy, the more determined we are not to expose the 'darker side' of our character.

We are usually at our most determined to portray positive images when we start a new job or take a new class for the first time. A new job may be seen as an opportunity for a clean break, a chance to wipe the slate clean and start again. However, over time, we may begin to recognize that we are falling back into our old ways of behaving. New surroundings and new colleagues may seduce us into believing things have changed, but often it is not long before our new circumstances begin to have an all too familiar ring to them.

Nelson-Jones (1983), in his highly readable book about counselling, also writes about the strategies people adopt to help them retain their preferred images of themselves. He calls these 'self-protective thinking'; they have also been referred to elsewhere as 'defence mechanisms' or 'security operations'. So people might *deny* the existence of uncomfortable feelings, *blame* others for things that go wrong instead of accepting any personal responsibility, *project* on to others things that they do not like about themselves, or *manipulate* so that it fits in with what is acceptable. These then are some of the ways in which we might react in order to preserve our self-image.

The third implication that arises from the notion of keeping some parts of ourselves 'behind a screen' relates to our choice of colleagues. We are drawn to those who resemble us in some way, not just for the behaviour they display but also for the behaviour they do not display. It is suggested that we actually sense what people have behind their screens, and this influences our decision about whether or not to spend time with them.

Let us summarize the discussion so far. How we respond to parental attributions and injunctions affects which emotions and situations make us feel comfortable and which do not. It determines which colleagues we spend time with and those we prefer to avoid or share very little with. Teachers have personal needs, desires, and established ways of behaving which determine how we relate to colleagues. What colleagues see of us, however, is what we might like to think is an idealized version of ourselves. What remains shielded from public view also contributes to how we interact in school and can lead us to adopt certain patterns of behaviour in order that all our needs are met.

Using this as our starting point, we can now move on to examine how staff or children might interact with each other, in order that they may get what they want from school life, not so much in a professional sense but at a more personal level, in terms of their undisclosed needs.

How do we interact with others?

Berne, in his well-known, popular psychology book *Games People Play* (Berne 1964), offered a framework through which interactions could be examined. He suggested individuals behave in ways which can be described as child-like, parent-like, or adult-like. Thus child-like behaviour is redolent of some aspects of behaviour learned during childhood. Parent-like behaviour represents aspects of behaviour we would usually associate with those of an individual's parents, and adult-like behaviour is indicated by references to objectivity and rationality rather than anything emotional.

Describing behaviour as child-, adult-, or parent-like is one way in which the behaviour of individual participants during an interaction can be represented. This analysis offers a means of looking at the unstated nature of interactions, particularly when those interactions are 'not straight', as one party desires an outcome which remains concealed.

Berne used these terms to examine relationships and the relative 'power' that participants exert during their interactions with each other. They provide the basis for examining the strategies that individuals might adopt in trying to get what they want, but without ever declaring their intentions. It is done in a somewhat deceptive manner and led Berne to describe the process as 'games people play'. We would now like to explore more fully the nature of interactions which are potentially negative (i.e., they are not straight) through considering the 'games *teachers* play'.

Games teachers play

One of the authors of this book has very clear memories of seeing Berne's book *Games People Play* lying around his home when a child. Being a sports enthusiast he naturally assumed it was related to this sphere of life. It was only some years later that the real content of the book became known and appreciated. However, in some senses the early inferences made about the book's contents are not entirely misplaced.

Although the games described are not those enjoyed by the sporting fraternity, they are played as seriously and with the same commitment to win, as the FA Cup Final, the Final of Wimbledon, or the climax to any other notable sporting encounter. Of course, with any sporting confrontation it is invariably clear that the participants are playing a game where there is a winner and loser. The nature of life's 'social games' are rarely spelled out so unequivocally.

The 'games people play' refers to interactions which we would term as 'not straight'. Berne defines a game as 'an ongoing series of complementary ulterior transactions to a well-defined, predictable outcome. Descriptively it is a recurring set of transactions, often repetitious, superficially plausible, with a concealed motivation' (Berne 1964:44). One or both participants in the interaction are concealing their motives. An important defining characteristic of any game is what is referred to as 'the pay-off'. What is to be gained by the various participants in the game? It is the desire and need for these pay-offs that spark off the game in the first place. Steiner defines games in similar terms:

> A game is a behavioural sequence which 1) is an orderly series of transactions with a beginning and an end; 2) contains an ulterior motive, that is, a psychological level different from the social level; and 3) results in a payoff for both players.
>
> (Steiner 1974:44)

We encounter games regularly in our lives. Consider the salesman who enquires after your health and personal well-being before getting down to the real business of selling you something. Nobody confuses the firm handshake and concerned questions about our health with the nature of their overall purpose. They are the social prelude to the more serious matter of selling a product. We may appreciate and perhaps allow ourselves to be persuaded by the rather superficial social interaction, but we still remain aware of its more serious psychological intent. The same happens around elections as political parties canvass for votes. The 'kissing baby' syndrome fools nobody, except perhaps the aspiring politician. They are out to win votes and the genteel social

139

charms displayed on the doorstep are designed with this obvious and specific ulterior motive.

Now these are fairly obvious examples of real motives remaining under wraps and the pay-off for the salesman or politician is very clear. Other games which can be a part of our interactions, both with adults and children, although following a similar course, are less obvious.

The purpose of our games relates to some very basic needs that we have. As young children we have particular physical and emotional needs for which we are reliant on our parents. As we grow older we have social needs which are possibly not met in the way we might have hoped. When this happens we may try alternative routes to get our basic needs met. Because they are not satisfied in a straightforward manner we resort to 'games' in an attempt to get what we want.

There is a range of games that may well be an integral part of everyday school life, particularly during stressful periods. Berne tried to convey the essence of the games he identified in a simple and readily understood way. He did so by describing each of them with a short phrase that he felt encapsulated their essential character and helped make them immediately recognizable. One is called 'see what you made me do'. Here the teacher may be engaged on a particular task and is interrupted by a child or member of staff causing some error on that task. The teacher's response is to feel that the intervention has led to the mistake and says, 'Now look what you've made me do'. The teacher disowns responsibility in this instance and attempts to locate it elsewhere. The game has implications for both parties: more obviously for the teacher denying responsibility, but also for the colleague or pupil who may, in the light of what happens, actually begin to feel responsible. This is more likely to happen in the case of a child than another teacher, but not necessarily so.

Another well-known game is 'why don't you – yes but' where one party poses a problem to which others offer solutions. However, every suggestion for overcoming the problem is greeted with the phrase 'yes but'. Eventually those offering remedies give up. The purpose of such a game for its instigator (behaving in a child-like manner) is not to find an 'adult solution' to the problem but to feel reassured that the potential solutions offered match those that they have already thought of. Those offering advice are cast in the role of 'parent' trying to find worthwhile and knowledgeable solutions. The poser of the problem leaves feeling victorious.

'Ain't it awful' is a game that most people will have encountered at some time in relation to teaching. It might be played in response to an ineffective lecturer, headteacher, or adviser, or arise in connection with a particular class and the difficulties they present. A group of teachers, seeking refuge in the pub one Friday lunchtime, despair at the headteacher's handling of a recent staff meeting. They assert that the way the school is run is deplorable and that the children behave like an undisciplined, unruly mob. The teachers contend that life in the school is 'awful'. The game allows its participants to disclaim responsibility for what happens because it's all the headteacher's fault.

These games have been described briefly in an attempt to give a flavour of the discourse when they are being played. Fuller descriptions and analyses of these games and others can be found in Berne (1964) and Steiner (1974). They do, we feel, illustrate the way in which what might appear to be 'adult-to-adult' interactions are undermined by a series of alternative and hidden motivations.

Easen (1985) also discusses games teachers play in his book about school-based, in-service training. Some of the games he highlights are called 'if only I had time'; 'she means well but'; and 'if it weren't for them' – titles which convey a sense of the scenarios they describe. He suggests they serve as barriers to effective communication between staff and considers how 'game playing' can be recognized and overcome.

Finally a brief word about the growing sociological literature on teachers' relationships with colleagues. It is based on ethnographic studies which have looked at the dynamics of school life and is a natural counterpoint to some of the ideas developed in this chapter. This literature provides another perspective on relationships in schools which complements those available from psychology. However, it has not been possible within the scope of this book to incorporate and do justice to these sociological perspectives.

In this chapter, the views offered represent a summary of some complex areas. We hope it has provided some insights into the nature of relationships and that it might encourage you to explore the ideas further. Our discussion is speculative. There is very little research from a psychological perspective that has looked at family and parental influences on teachers and the impact this might have on practice. As games theory presents a somewhat pessimistic, and some might say cynical, perspective on human behaviour, in the next chapter we present an alternative, positive view on the course interactions might take in the class and staffroom.

Chapter Eleven

Straight communications

In earlier chapters we expressed a desire for others in the education system to be more open in their dealings with the teaching profession. In addition we suggested it was important that teachers themselves retained a critical and healthy scepticism concerning educational rhetoric and exhortations to teach in certain ways.

We would now like to consider how teachers might bring a similar openness to their own practice in their relationship with colleagues, parents, and children. In essence our concerns are similar to others (for example Carr and Kemmis 1986; Pollard and Tann 1987; Stenhouse 1975) who, in their differing ways, have urged teachers to reflect on their own practice and to be willing to find their own answers to questions and problems, rather than rely on the edicts of 'experts'. Our request to teachers is simple, and some might say naïve, namely to be straight in their interactions with others and, equally important, straight with themselves.

Beginning to negotiate and being straight results not from changing the behaviour of others but from reflecting critically on our own behaviour. Looking at the nature of our contact with others and how this makes us feel, provides a starting point when working towards straight communications with colleagues, parents, and children. We may have persistent blind spots, but a willingness to accept responsibility for the quality of our relationships will at least provide a starting point from which to begin.

How then might it be possible to work towards being more open in our professional role as teachers?

Getting on your own map

Skynner and Cleese introduce the notion of 'being on your own map' as providing the impetus for healthy, straight interactions. They look at how children develop and the crucial role parents play as children grow older. One of the fundamental responsibilities of parenthood is to help children appreciate their own position in the world relative to other people.

New-born babies are dependent on parents for everything. When they cry, parents invariably respond immediately, which conveys to children the impression that their parents are at their continual beck and call. It is suggested that children develop a sense of omnipotence, a feeling which, if it persists, is far from positive. Life cannot always revolve round children in this way and it is up to parents to help them understand the real limits of their effective control over others.

As children grow older, they try to work out what their relationships are with significant people in their lives. This gradual process of recognizing that others also have desires, needs, and preferences, which may compete with their own but are equally valid, is referred to as 'getting on your own map'. Being on your own map implies a recognition that others have opinions and rights and that, when they conflict with yours, they can be resolved through discussion and negotiation.

'Being on your own map' has a number of implications. The first concerns your attitudes and relationships with those in positions of authority. It is suggested that you are less likely to occupy the extreme positions of rebel or being rigid, obsessional, and over-controlled. You are able to work in a team and accept the views of colleagues and the decisions reached. Equally, if in a position of authority yourself, you would exercise your responsibilities in a fair and democratic manner. You would listen to a range of opinions, facilitate discussion, and finally make decisions, the rationale for which you would explain.

A second implication of 'being on your own map' relates to how you, as a teacher, are able to respond to the social needs of pupils. The personal educational philosophies of many teachers involve actively promoting children's social development, and it is also a fundamental part of the writings of many educationalists. However, it is debatable how successfully this role can be fulfilled by teachers who are not 'on their own map', or remain unaware that they may be screening off what they find uncomfortable. In such circumstances how might teachers promote group and class discussions, or collaborative working amongst children? Similarly, how might they respond to children who behave in ways that they have difficulty in accepting themselves? Let us stay with this latter area and return to a theme developed in Chapter Nine, when we looked at perceptions of 'disruptive behaviour'.

One of the responsibilities of parents is to help children learn socially acceptable forms of behaviour. As we have already stated, children are initially egocentric and think they are the centre of the universe with life revolving around them. Parents enable their children to adopt a more realistic view, through laying down rules and outlining the boundaries of acceptable social behaviour. Recognizing you cannot have everything your own way is a painful but essential lesson to learn. However, what happens if children come to school and have never learned this? Let us suppose their parents always gave in to them at the merest hint of a tantrum. It may come as quite a shock to such children, on arrival at school, to find that they cannot do just as they like, that there are social conventions to be followed, and that the needs of other children have to be considered as well as their own.

As we stated in Chapters Seven and Eight, we regard labelling children 'disruptive' under these circumstances as saying more about the teacher and how she reacts to a situation, than anything about children. Will a teacher who interprets behaviour in this manner be in a position to help put children 'on their own map', so they can appreciate that they cannot have their own way all the time?

Although the process of helping pupils to recognize their status in relation to peers may present difficulties for both teachers and child, it is a necessary stage for a child's healthy emotional and social development. What happens to children who always get what they want, whose parents or teachers avoid tackling the problem because they choose not to deal with a display of temper or displeasure? Children have to learn to cope with a range of uncomfortable emotions such as jealousy or envy or competitiveness. Will a teacher who has screened off these emotions be able to respond to the needs of children expressing such feelings? We think not. Teachers 'being on their own map' has, in our view, a significant bearing on the extent to which they will be able to work with colleagues and to facilitate children's social and emotional development.

Acknowledging our own feelings

There is one further implication of 'being on our own map' and recognizing that we place feelings that we find uncomfortable behind the screen. These are the traits we tend to project onto others and deny displaying ourselves. Our descriptions of colleagues behaving in ways of which we do not approve may be a reflection of what we have difficulty in coming to terms with about our own behaviour. It is the emotions we try not to display that are likely to be the ones we project on to others.

However, when we acknowledge that we are not perfect, that we behave in ways we do not always like, and experience emotions we find uncomfortable and would prefer to ignore, we have a firmer basis from which to negotiate. We are less likely to accuse our colleagues of interacting in ways which mirror how we feel, but prefer to disregard, in order to protect our preferred images of ourselves.

Hearing as well as listening

By four o'clock on most busy schooldays, many teachers will feel that they have spent a fair amount of time listening to children talk. Children will want to discuss personal revelations, topics that have captured their imagination, and to share new discoveries. It is also fairly likely that they will want to tell tales about their friends, complain that the work is boring or too hard, and enquire whether football is still on following last night's rain. It is all part and parcel of school life. A teacher will have 'listened' to a lot each day but how much will have been 'heard'.

Within the language of interpersonal communicating, the verb 'to hear' has acquired a meaning which implies more than just listening. It infers that what you listen to is understood and acknowledged in the way the speaker intended. It is, if you like, simply recognizing what has been said, without trying to change it in any way through reinterpretation. (This concept is sometimes referred to as 'active listening'.)

Given the increasing pressures on teachers, many inevitably regret feeling unable to give enough time to each child in their class. When teachers are engaged in conversations with their pupils, how much individual attention is a teacher able to give? How feasible is it to 'hear', as well as 'listen', to what children are saying? Similarly when talking with colleagues, how much is actually heard of what they say? When topics are raised for discussion, to what extent do participants reflect their understanding of what others have said, or do they merely restate their own views in a number of different ways?

We raise this issue because it is very easy to fail to hear what children or colleagues are saying, and so inadvertently leave them in a position where they feel that the listener is not interested in what they have to relate. To some extent though, children need to learn that within the social context of the classroom they cannot always have the attention they would like, just when they want it. It is a necessary social lesson and part of learning to 'get on your own map'.

Such a situation can be contrasted with the occasions when children feel they have a genuine need for a teacher's attention. How teachers respond to this will depend on the general circumstances prevailing in the classroom at the time.

Acknowledging and not discounting the feelings of children

Imagine another school scenario. At the end of playtime the teacher walks back to the classroom. She is waiting for the children when they return from the playground. As they come in, one pupil appears upset and makes her way over to the teacher. She looks red-faced and tearful and tries to recount the details of a playtime event she found distressing.

145

The teacher intends getting the lesson off to a brisk start and does not want to get side-tracked into dealing with the issues raised by the pupil. After listening to the pupil she turns to her and says 'Well never mind, you shouldn't let that upset you, go to your place and get ready for the next lesson'.

Such a response, from the teacher's point of view, may be understandable but effectively dismisses the way the child may be feeling. This occurs, not because of the brevity of her remarks and her desire to start the lesson, but rather because she is discounting the feelings of the child. In telling the child she shouldn't feel upset, the teacher is adding her own interpretation to the child's account of events and judging that what has happened does not warrant the child's tearful response. The teacher has listened to what the pupil has said but has not appreciated it from the child's point of view. The teacher has not heard what the child has said, nor recognized the validity of the child's feelings and reaction to a distressing situation. The child's behaviour has not been accepted unconditionally by the teacher. Instead it has been judged, in this instance, as an inappropriate response to the events which preceded it.

Such an interaction serves to undermine children through dismissing and discounting their personal feelings and emotions. In spite of the teacher's concerns with the other children and wanting to start the lesson, she could have managed the matter differently and achieved her goals without undermining the child. For example, she might have said, 'I'm not surprised you're feeling upset. Let's talk about what happened after this lesson when we've both got some time'.

On occasions there is a similar tendency to discount the feelings and concerns of parents. Parents may go up to school if they are worried about their child's progress, but may meet with a response that illustrates how their views can be all too readily dismissed. After expressing their anxieties, parents may be told by a teacher not to worry, that there is nothing wrong, and that everything is all right. These comments effectively dismiss parents' perceptions and potentially deceive them, if, as frequently happens, some of those children, at a future date, are felt to be failing and making unsatisfactory progress. We have met a number of parents in such a position, whose initial concerns are now tinged with feelings of anger at having being misled.

So how might a teacher avoid such interactions with children, parents, and colleagues? As we have indicated, the teacher in our first example would recognize the pupil's feelings and acknowledge them to the child. Then at some mutually convenient time, chat to the child to find some way of dealing with the difficulties that have been created. Similarly, in relation to parents, it would be helpful to recognize their perceptions and to discuss ways of proceeding in the future that reflect how they are feeling. And so it would also be with colleagues. In fact there are a number of approaches to working in groups to solve problems, where the starting point for those involved is for everyone to state their own views before inviting questions to clarify what is suggested. It is only at some later stage, when individual positions have been heard and understood, that discussion moves on to tackle differences.

Discounting the feelings, opinions, and attitudes of children whether by parents or teachers, is a powerful process. It is all part of inducting children into the life script termed by Steiner as 'mindlessness'. Here the child's perceptions of life and the world are frequently invalidated by adult comments which leave the child feeling confused, anxious, and lacking in self-belief.

The issues raised here highlight the importance of 'being straight' during interactions with colleagues, parents, and children; the concept is embodied within the position of 'I'm OK, you're OK'. Relating to others as equals removes the need to conceal information you think others might find uncomfortable or unwelcome and which invariably provides a platform for games playing.

Asking for what we want

We have considered in some detail how our behaviour and that of children may be bound by the life scripts we follow. The attributions and injunctions we receive create our expectations for life. They shape our perceptions and prepare us to accept that we are not entitled to certain things, which, however, are available to others. We may want greater recognition from our headteacher or colleagues for our efforts. Or we might want feedback from children on a particular lesson. It is from such a starting point that people embark on games. They do not get what they desire during the normal course of events and so use games to obtain these pay-offs.

There may, therefore, be things that we want from our personal and professional lives but which we do not feel we have any right to expect. And so it may be with children. They too may desire certain outcomes from school life but do not feel entitled to them. If we are committed to more open relationships, we can begin to ask for what we want and similarly encourage children to do the same. The alternative is either not to have the things we wish for, or to resort to games in order to get them. However, asking for what we want does not automatically guarantee that we receive it, but ensures that our desires are aired openly and not concealed and repackaged in less straight interactions.

There is another side to asking for what we want. We have noted a tendency for people (ourselves included) to try to work out from the behaviour of others what they want. We see what they do, listen to what they have to say, and if we are not sure what they are getting at, effectively feel forced into trying to read their minds to work out what they desire. This is especially so when there is a mismatch between what people say and do. We then try to generate our own solutions to explain their actions. It may well be that at such times we are in danger of being drawn into playing games. When we are not sure of someone else's aims and motives, we can play it straight and ask them directly what they want.

We can also be open with children and state what we expect from them, especially in terms of their classroom behaviour and their attitude to work. Again our impression is that many teachers have clear expectations of children in both these areas. However, they are rarely stated explicitly to children, who are expected to know what is required of them but are not told what this is. They are, therefore, in the unenviable position of having to work out for themselves what the teacher regards as acceptable.

As we have already noted, school can be a bemusing place for children, especially in contrast to their home environment. During their school lives they come into contact with many teachers whose expectations may vary considerably. Children can be helped to make sense of these varying requirements if teachers are more direct in asking them to behave in particular ways.

Giving permission

Linked to asking for what we want is the concept of giving yourself, and others, permission to behave in ways which run counter to parental injunctions and attributions. Because these are so powerful and established over many years, we have effectively to go through a process of saying to ourselves that we can do things which contradict potent family and societal messages. We can also give children permission to behave in ways which conflict with their own expectations.

One area where adults and children receive similarly powerful attributions and injunctions is in relation to gender roles. Males and females are assigned specific roles in society, although these have been increasingly challenged in recent times. Boys are told they must be brave or strong, whereas girls are to be gentle or dependent. A teacher can, at the appropriate times, give boys and girls permission to behave in ways not associated with their gender. So when a boy is feeling upset, he can be given permission to cry and be told it is all right to do so. Equally, girls can be told it is OK to be assertive and ask for what they want. They do not have to take second place to boys and adopt their designated role. By giving others permission to behave in certain ways we can pre-empt any inclination they have to embark on playing games to meet their needs.

Asking straight questions

A final feature of straight communications that we highlight concerns asking 'straight questions' and is discussed in more detail in the next chapter. What is our purpose in asking questions? Why do we phrase them one way rather than another? Is it to seek information or opinions, or are there other factors which prompt us to adopt a particular line of enquiry? The questions we ask play an important role in how we share our perceptions of the world and negotiate knowledge, themes raised earlier in the book and brought together in the final chapter. We therefore discuss asking 'straight questions', in relation to these broader issues, in Chapter Twelve.

At this point we feel we have come full circle. For teachers to behave in the way we are suggesting requires that they are aware of attributions and injunctions in their own lives which determine the emotions they place in front of or behind their screens. A teacher who is unwilling to recognize that her behaviour may be very much influenced by gender stereotyping is unlikely to be in a position to facilitate a child's social development, particularly in relation to gender roles.

What we have described is the personal counterpoint to teachers questioning the formal education system in which they are asked to play a part. If they reflect on their own behaviour, their values, and beliefs in a critical manner, they are more likely to engage in open and straight communications with colleagues, parents, and children. They are more likely to hear what others say and they are more likely to recognize that their own perceptions of the world are personal stories which are the basis for discussion than rather definitive statements of truth.

Part IV

This final section contains just one chapter. In it, we summarize the way our analysis of influence on the teacher has progressed through the book. We look more closely at what we think are the implications of the teacher becoming empowered. A major theme in the book, the process of negotiation, is given more consideration. We argue that knowledge should be viewed as tentative and negotiated, rather than certain and imposed. We also argue for an interpersonal stance that cuts away the games playing. We acknowledge the seeming vulnerability for the teacher in following this line, but argue for its effectiveness in helping resist the many influences exerted by the educational system and people within it.

Chapter Twelve

Inspiring teachers

Is there a code to crack?

This chapter aims to take the themes of the preceding chapters and to weave them into a pattern that relates to the individual teacher and the process of teaching. The book has explored, in turn, elements of the educational system and features of organizations that have a major bearing on the work of teachers. As well as these external influences, our perspective has recognized the potential of personal factors to influence what teachers do in schools and in the classroom. In particular, we have paid attention to the views of some psychologists, who emphasize the way our upbringing can provide us with the pattern or 'script' for our adult lives and mould our values.

We have covered ground in this book that has touched on ethical and moral issues. There have been themes to do with self-knowledge; with using language to communicate rather than to deceive; with becoming aware of rituals and myths; and with the nature of power in the organization and control of education.

Our intention has been to encourage teachers to feel more in control of their own professional practice and we have used the term 'empowering' to refer to this process. All around them, teachers witness the effects of changes in so many aspects of their professional lives. Approaches to discipline have changed; the curriculum keeps on changing; the government of schools is changing; new ways of assessing pupils are being introduced; in-service training for teachers has become a major enterprise; and the government is thinking of ways of changing initial training for teachers. Some teachers view what is happening to education in the same way as one might view open-cast mining in a National Park; except that for them, the devastation is not happening in some remote part of the countryside but within their own backyard. It is their jobs that are being affected, their pupils, their schools.

Teachers need all the support that they can get and if our intention were solely to do that, then we would be pursuing a justifiable objective.

But we wish to do more than that. We have set out to encourage teachers to look at themselves, at their teaching, at their school, and at the educational system from an analytical stance. Sometimes, we have offered a broad overview of an area; in parts, we have presented a more detailed analysis. We recognize that we have not approached our subject matter with a consistency of depth. However, our purpose is to prompt the reader into analysing her own teaching, rather than to provide the definitive analysis. In this sense, there is no universal code for teaching waiting to be cracked, only, perhaps, our own personal codes. One of the implicit themes of this book has been a doubtfulness about prescription. The future *is* unknown for each of us. Today's analysis is to prepare us for tomorrow's uncertainty.

Do we have a type of teacher in mind?

In this chapter, we seek to explore what kind of teachers might pursue the sort of reflective, enquiring approach to their work that we have been talking about. We also consider the implications of following some of the ideas that we have expressed.

Postman and Weingartner (1969) talk about 'crap-detecting'. What sort of a teacher is a successful crap-detector? We have made the case for teachers to recognize their own propaganda, to strip away the layers of defence that protect them from the slings and arrows of interpersonal misfortune. Everything that has been advocated in this book so far leaves the teacher exposed and vulnerable.

For the reader who follows our line, there can be no undeserved authority, no automatic ritual, no practice that is accepted as valid other than as a working hypothesis. For such teachers, there can be no comfort in the certainty of routine. Doubt is the customary state of mind and questioning the customary mode. This is potentially very debilitating and must seem a long way from helping teachers to combat feelings of powerlessness. How can leaving the teacher to stand alone against the collective wisdom of colleagues, or against the authority of the educational establishment, be empowering? There will necessarily be much that the teacher has to take on trust. Being doubtful *and* trusting? Yes, we think it is possible to be both. We think that to survive as a teacher it is necessary to be optimistic, both about people, especially children, and about the power of education for positive change.

The trusting teacher?

This optimism involves trust in others, in their motives, in their veracity. At the same time, an eye must be kept open for undue influence, for those who seek to exercise illegitimate control. This blend of being both open and street-wise at the same time is no easy thing to attain. In fact, you could argue that it is considerably more difficult than taking a sceptical view of educational practice. Scepticism does at.least provide a suit of armour, a defensive attitude from which to survey the world. To be doubting is not so difficult if one is permitted to distance oneself from others. But we are suggesting trust in others as an opening gambit.

Starting from an open and trusting position, however, does not remove the need to be alert to signs of hidden agendas and games that may occur. The skill is not so much in spotting what might be happening as you interact with someone, as in having the ability to check out with that person just what is going on. If, for example, what you think the other person is saying is making you feel angry, you need to to acknowledge how you are feeling and to check out whether you are understanding what was meant. The situation needs to be confronted in a way that permits both of you to make as much progress as possible. This is no easy way out of the dilemma of interactions that cause you discomfort and, as we said early on in the book, what we suggest is not necessarily comfortable, although it is positive.

If you have spent time considering what is behind your screen, are you enfeebled or empowered? Our argument is, of course, that self-knowledge is a strength, that with such knowledge you are less easily blown off course. This is not to argue for psychoanalysis, but that an awareness of the things that wind you up, or that you avoid, can give you some power over yourself.

Cracking your own code

The process of getting in touch with yourself is no easy process. It can take a long time and may necessitate many different ways of trying to achieve it before you begin to make progress. In the sense that Kelly (1977) views scientific progress as possibly being an artefact of different ways of construing the same phenomena, so progress towards self-knowledge might be a similar process of reconstruing one's own experience. It might be that the process of searching is more important than what you find. This might sound like promotion of oriental philosophy (and perhaps it is!), but to be aware of your own values and where they come from, makes it possible for you to be clear with other people what your views are.

By clarifying your values, you are in a better position to listen honestly to other people. By being able to declare your values, you are modelling an openness in communication with others. In such circumstances, discussion should be able to proceed without any elaborate games playing. If the purpose of an interaction is to exchange meaning in a straightforward manner, it is likely that the declaration of values, relevant to the discussion, will help to make the interaction worthwhile.

Is it naïve, this idea that unilaterally we should expose to others our values and views? Psychologically speaking, are we not most vulnerable when we remove some of the layers of defences that we have built up around us? Are these defences not the result of many years of experience in the world? Well, there may indeed be considerable justification in asking these questions. No doubt, our games playing and social interactional subterfuges have some survival value, not least in temporarily reducing our anxiety. The problem is that we defend ourselves by protecting our core constructs from being invalidated. We avoid experiences which contradict our way of viewing the world. We do not seek disconfirmatory evidence, but, instead, look for experiences or people with a propensity for confirming what we already think we know. The question is whether we feel truly more in control, more empowered, by keeping hidden our values and our constructs.

Protecting our games plan?

It might seem like a source of strength to keep our games strategies out of sight. And so it is, if the purpose of social interaction is adversarial. If every social encounter is seen as a battle to be won, then weapons might be needed, and probably secret ones at that. It is unlikely that anyone involved in teaching would view the world in such a way. To anyone viewing the world with such hostility, our advice would be to choose another occupation. To be in charge of young people, to influence their emotional and social development while having such an untrusting view of others would be damaging for those young people and a nightmare for the teacher.

Perhaps we have taken an extreme example, however, and you might feel inclined to ask whether it would not make more sense to be partially open about your values. Perhaps it is possible to be guarded – not entirely secretive in one's values but not entirely forthcoming either? Is this multilateral disarmament? You expose something of your values and I'll expose something of mine? At first sight, this looks like straight negotiation and so it might be if we declare at the outset that this is what we are doing. But, on reflection, one is bound to recognize that the potential for misunderstanding is present in any approach when you begin an interaction as a bargaining exercise. The chances are considerable of one party feeling aggrieved if the balance of trade ends up not in their favour.

Another point needs to be made, however, about the extent of the openness required for straightforward communication. It is difficult to isolate exclusively the underpinning values that are relevant to any particular communication topic. When we engage in discussion, it is difficult to know precisely where we should draw the boundaries around those areas of our values that we are willing to disclose. There is scope in this for us to go on disclosing more information than is needed to enhance the meaning of the interaction. Where do we stop?

How can we share our values?

Each interaction cannot begin with the participants issuing a long statement about their creed. No business would ever get done. So how do you decide when enough is enough? This is not a process that can be governed by any simple formula or procedure. The answer has to be that for straight communication to occur, each participant needs to alert the other to those values, beliefs, constructs, or views which underpin the argument or evidence being put forward. There will be a point in the discussion when a person becomes aware that to withhold information about their values is to mislead the other person. At this point, it is better to admit to some discomfort and negotiate with the other an opportunity to explain one's position.

So far we have laid great store by negotiation as a fundamental principle in social interaction. It is worth looking again at this process and elaborating further what we mean by negotiation.

Negotiating knowledge

We have taken the view that knowledge itself becomes a social phenomenon as soon as we seek to transmit it to others. Knowledge is not neutral. It is selected from a massive array of possible data according to how we choose to collect it. Knowledge may be further processed according to how we wish to transmit it. Perhaps it is an inherent characteristic of the process of making sense of information, and, indeed, of the process of trying to make evidence sensible to others that we distort the data. It is partly in recognition of this distortion that we think knowledge is to be negotiated. To pretend that we have some means of acquiring truth – facts or views which demand universal acceptance – is to exert some form of social influence over those whom we wish to receive such truth.

As an aside, so far we have presented knowledge as a social phenomenon in respect of it being transmitted to others. It is possible to pursue a stronger argument, namely that all knowledge, private as well as public, is socially determined, since the data-collecting framework that determines our personal processes is an internalized version of a social framework, drawn from our social interactional experience. It is thus possible to argue that the abstraction of information from the world is done in accordance with models about the world that have been socially determined.

Whether or not one adopts this stronger account of knowledge being socially determined, the argument remains valid that to transmit evidence to others is to participate in an information-handling process in which we need to make sense of the evidence ourselves and then anticipate the sense that others will also make of the data. Evidence does not carry an automatic right to be believed. You are not obliged to believe it. Indeed, you are not obliged to believe this view that we are putting forward (and there's an interesting paradox!). The likely distortion of knowledge in the process of transmission is, however, not the only reason for us to argue for the negotiation of knowledge. We also take the view that knowledge can be used to exert undue influence – to manipulate others.

Using knowledge to influence others

Here we need to say what we mean by undue or illegitimate influence and what sort of influence is legitimate. Already in the discussion on language, we have declared that language can be used for all sorts of purposes in interaction. We have also explained about the need to declare those of our values that are relevant when attempting to communicate in a straightforward manner. By undue or illegitimate influence, we mean any attempt to invalidate the views of another by making claims for the knowledge that one has, only with the intention of disadvantaging the other. The methods of making such claims can be subtle indeed. However, it is likely that one uses knowledge in argument as a means of invalidating the opinion of others, if one subscribes to a prescriptive view of knowledge as being a cultural store to which some people have more access than others.

It is possible to hold a different view of knowledge. Instead of a store of garnered facts, we might view knowledge as a collection of tools that are judged by their usefulness. These tools wear out or can be used to make new or more specialized tools. Clearly, the view that teachers have about knowledge may substantially influence their approach to teaching. If knowledge is seen as a commodity to be given to learners, it opens up the way for education to be seen as propaganda – someone has decided what the learner shall know, or not know. And yet there will be knowledge that teachers want to give to learners and must it all be classed as propaganda? We see propaganda as an extreme form of undue influence and education as being a legitimate use of influence.

To use the concept of continua again, it is possible to see propaganda and education as being at opposite ends of a continuum representing influence. If the teacher limits the opportunity of the student to challenge the knowledge he or she presents – by, for example, deliberately omitting information about a different perspective – then that, for us, represents undue influence and moves near to propaganda. Propaganda, itself, however, might be seen as the use of deliberately designed material and arguments to sway the opinions of others. As teachers move away from presenting knowledge as precious gems from society's cultural treasure trove towards a view of knowledge as a tool that can be replaced when necessary, then the scope for undue influence is diminished.

You may be thinking that there are facts, data about the world, that you consider irrefutable. Indeed it would be foolish not to recognize that there are ways of making sense of the world that people share in common. In Chapter Four, we drew attention to the fact that Schutz offers a way of dealing with the problem of how to make progress if each of us sees the world from a unique standpoint. Schutz's thesis permits us to make assumptions about perspectives that we might have in common with others, so that we can make progress without having to check every detail of our joint experience.

Ralf Dahrendorf has argued for the idea that knowledge requires public scrutiny. In an essay entitled 'Uncertainty, Science and Democracy', he proposed a 'principle of uncertainty'. Dahrendorf wrote:

> Our only protection from bad science and from the dogmas of false science lies in the mutual criticism of practising scientists. Science is always a concert, a contrapuntal chorus of the many who are engaged in it. Insofar as truth exists at all, it exists not as a possession of the individual scholar, but as the net result of scientific interchange.

> (Dahrendorf 1968:242–3)

Dahrendorf in the same chapter goes on to argue against 'exercises in objectivity with the help of psychoanalysis and the sociology of knowledge'. He argues against the idea that objectivity can be obtained by training, and puts forward the view that knowledge proceeds through open debate. This is consistent with the view that we have expressed in the sense that when we advocate self-awareness, we are not arguing in favour of an unrealizable objectivity, but to recognize the fundamental nature of our subjectivity and its inseparability from what we know and how we communicate.

Another point of agreement with Dahrendorf is the view that knowledge progresses through a social process. Knowledge is legitimized through social acceptance and to be thus accepted it needs to run the gauntlet of enquiry and questioning. For Dahrendorf, the social dialectics are a safer way of determining the progress of science than an appeal to the objectivity of the scientist. However, we would still argue that the process of social dispute or dialectics is fundamentally a dispute about values. How we question the evidence or views of others, and the sorts of questions that we ask, reveal our values.

Knowledge and subcultural membership

It follows from what we have been saying, that there are levels of understanding which must be negotiated. It requires no detailed search of anthropological literature to discover that facts cherished by one culture are not necessarily recognized by another. Indeed, membership of a culture may depend on the extent to which one believes in a view of the world which coincides with how other members of that culture view the world. The same process may determine the membership of sub-cultures in our society. For example, what are the beliefs that are required for you to 'belong' to that group of primary school educators who are influenced by the Plowden Report? Moreover, as we discussed in Chapter Seven, orthodoxy of beliefs may, to a large part, be a question of how language is used. Here again, we have departed from a level of knowledge that can be held more commonly within our culture to the point at which subgroups can be culturally differentiated.

Perhaps, therefore, another way of defining illegitimate influence, is that it involves the power of group membership, symbolized by belief in particular values and 'facts', being used against another person. This is achieved by suggesting or implying that particular beliefs and facts are supported by the group. It is a psychological process, whereby the more people are supposed to believe particular evidence or hold particular views, the harder it is for the individual to stand against such influence.

It is in recognition of the power that can be exercised in the name of knowledge, facts, or evidence, that we would emphasize the value of negotiation and the recognition by participants that the status of evidence itself must be jointly agreed.

Giving up the power of knowledge

Having required of our readers that they reveal their values as part of straight communication, are we now requiring them to give up their knowledge base, to put their evidence on the table to be discussed as to its mutual acceptability? The straight answer is 'yes'. If we do not recognize that the evidence that we value so highly may not be acceptable to the other person, we are acting as if we have an automatically superior route to the 'truth', as if the oracle has spoken only to us.

What we are not suggesting is that we give up our beliefs or our values. A declaration of what we believe is a statement about our fundamental values. Whilst our values must respond to legitimate influence, in the sense of being 'working values', this is not at the same level as being prepared to negotiate about data, or evidence, or knowledge. The important distinction in practice is that of recognizing when a discussion is about values and when it is about evidence.

If, as we advocate, people declare their values in respect of some area of discussion, then this paves the way for a debate about values *as* values, rather than a discussion in which values are encoded in other formats, such as data, received wisdom, knowledge, or evidence. There is no suggestion by us that people should not have ideals, nor that they should not keep faith with themselves. As we see it, the confident teacher strikes a balance between feeling that they are 'in the driving seat' and negotiating with those around, including colleagues, parents, and students. Their openness to information and their lack of pre-emption makes such teachers particularly capable of negotiating in a flexible manner and having values that are subjected to disconfirmatory experience.

Straight questions

Another feature of negotiating with others concerns how we use questions. Increasing self-awareness involves knowing why you asked one kind of question rather than another. The art of questioning within straight communication is not easy. A question is a form of probe into the mental life of another person. Take a simple question: 'What did you do yesterday evening?'. Now the answers to that are many, since without both context and intention on the part of the questioner being made clear, the question can have very different interpretations.

Supposing, in the example above, the questioner is an irate father talking to his teenage son, following a phone call from the police about an incident. Or suppose the father is joining his son in the garage where the lad is restoring a motor bike with his father's supervision and advice. Or simply, the family are having breakfast together and the father is making a polite opening remark. We need not elaborate but you can work out for yourself a host of different responses to this same question. Each time the person being asked the question is trying to work out what the question means – what is the 'real' question being asked.

For straight communication, the questioner needs to help this process by declaring what the question is really about. Indeed, one could go a stage further if one is to avoid the abuse of power in an unequal relationship and give the reason for asking the question in order to give the listener real choice about answering. One might also make it acceptable not to answer. Being empowered gives the teacher the confidence to not assume power over those who are not empowered, these being typically the students with whom she works.

Returning briefly to the 'what did you do yesterday evening' question, let us suppose that this question is being asked by a teacher with pastoral responsibility, following information from a parent that the student had not gone home the previous night. To ask this question legitimately, the teacher would need to explain to the student why the question was being asked and what the teacher would do with the answer. If the teacher does not set out the parameters to the questioning, it is impossible for the student to know what is going on. The way in which we provide to others the framework in which we ask them questions helps to ensure that they know where our questioning is leading.

Undoubtedly, the context in which we ask questions also determines whether a particular question is straight or not. If the student is being asked questions in a court, he or she knows that the purpose of the court is to determine someone's guilt or innocence on a charge. In such circumstances, there are legal procedures that limit the type of questions that may be put, but generally all parties are aware of what the proceedings are about.

To be questioned by another in ordinary conversation is to operate under rules that are less clear than in a court of law. The empowered teacher will seek to avoid questioning another for an undisclosed purpose. The ends do not justify the means. For us to engage in interactions with others in a way that attempts to invalidate them serves only to invalidate ourselves ultimately. To stand against being drawn into confrontational games requires a lot of personal strength and some insight into ourselves.

Becoming empowered

The empowered teacher has spent time cracking her own code, looking at what is behind her screen, at what script she is using in her life, at what influences she has received. Without undue concentration on herself, she has attempted to make sense of who she is, why she views the world in the way she does, and why she has entered teaching. This process of self-awareness is not an indulgence nor has it a final product. There is a danger that people might confuse a narcissistic preoccupation with oneself with real self-awareness that is aimed at making more effective one's communications and relationships with others.

The process of self-awareness continues throughout one's life and is characterized by a willingness to re-examine experience and to re-live one's part in social interactions. It is a process that requires us to re-evaluate our world and to revalue it. Keeping faith with oneself does not mean hanging on doggedly to what one believes in the face of disconfirmatory experience. It does mean not shifting for the sake of social conformity. It also means viewing evidence as being value-ridden. This does not invalidate that evidence since, as we have argued, all evidence reflects values of one sort or another. It requires an approach to influence from others that is both open and questioning.

Equipped with self-awareness; being open-minded about people, their values, and their evidence; holding a personal understanding of the world that accepts disconfirmatory evidence and can change accordingly; the empowered teacher models a way of approaching new experience for her students. She checks on the language she uses and that the message received is the one intended.

Basically, she declares her faith in the humanizing value of education and works towards that. She is quite clear that it *is* a faith, that there is not necessarily evidence to support or disconfirm that view and that she must explain to others where she is starting from in terms of her values. She finds that as a teacher she is required to play a large number of roles. Sometimes she finds she is expected to offer counselling; sometimes she has to act as arbiter between students; sometimes, she finds the job requires police work. She is called on to be an observer, a critic, a philosopher, a researcher, an economist, a token 'responsible adult', a dispenser of wisdom, comfort, and security. Sometimes she is called on to be an educationalist, having views about the best way forward for education as a whole and for that part over which she has control. In all of this, she finds that the process of knowing who she is, why she views the world in the way that she does, and her belief in the humanizing value of education stand her in good stead. Not only does she survive but, to the extent that education can reach them, so do the generations of students that she teaches.

References

Adams, D. (1984) *So Long, and Thanks for All the Fish*, London: Pan.

Alexander, R.J. (1984) *Primary Teaching*, London: Cassell.

Atkinson, J.M. (1984) *Our Masters' Voices: The Language and Body Language of Politics*, London: Methuen.

Ball, S.J. and Goodson, I.F. (1985) *Teachers' Lives and Careers*, Lewes: Falmer Press.

Barker-Lunn, J. (1984) 'Junior school teachers: their methods and practices', in *Educational Research*, 26, 3: 178–88.

Barrow, R. (1984) *Giving Teaching Back to Teachers*, Sussex: Wheatsheaf.

Bennett, N., Deforges, C., Cockburn, A., and Wilkinson, B. (1984) *The Quality of Pupil Learning Experiences*, London: Lawrence Erlbaum Associates.

Berne, E. (1964) *Games People Play*, Harmondsworth: Penguin.

Blenkin, G.V. and Kelly, A.V. (1987) *The Primary Curriculum: A Process Approach to Curriculum Planning*, London: Harper & Row.

Blyth, W.A.L. (1984) *Development, Experience, and Curriculum in Primary Education*, London: Croom Helm.

Blyth, W.A.L. (1988) 'Bases for the primary curriculum', in M. Clarkson (ed.) *Emerging Issues in Primary Education*, Lewes: Falmer Press.

Bronowski, J. (1960) *The Common Sense of Science*, Harmondsworth: Penguin.

Brown, J.A.C. (1954) *The Social Psychology of Industry*, Harmondsworth: Penguin.

Bull, S.L. and Solity, J.E. (1987) *Classroom Management: Principles to Practice*, London: Croom Helm.

CACE (Central Advisory Council for Education [England]) (1967) *Children and their Primary Schools*, (the Plowden Report) 2 Vols, London: HMSO.

Campbell, R.J. (1985) *Developing the Primary School Curriculum*, London: Cassell.

Carr, W. and Kemmis, S. (1986) *Becoming Critical*, Lewes: Falmer Press.

Carrington, B. and Troyna, B. (1988) *Children and Controversial Issues*, Lewes: Falmer Press.

Cheeseman, P.L. and Watts, P.E. (1985) *Positive Behaviour Management*, London: Croom Helm.

Child, D. (1981) *Psychology and the Teacher*, London: Holt, Rinehart & Winston.

Child, D. (1985) 'Educational psychology: past, present and future', in N. Entwistle (ed.) *New Directions in Educational Psychology: 1 Learning and Teaching*, Lewes: Falmer Press.

Child, D. (1986) *Psychology and the Teacher*, London: Cassell (Fourth Edition).

Child, D. (1986) *Applications of Psychology for the Teacher*, London: Cassell.

Clarke, A.M. and Clarke A.D.B. (1976) *Early Experience: Myth and Evidence*, London: Open Books.

Cohen, A. and Cohen, L. (eds) (1986) *Primary Education: A Sourcebook For Teachers*, London: Harper & Row.

Combs, A.W. (1979) *Myths in Education: Beliefs that Hinder Progress and their Alternatives*, London: Allyn & Bacon.

Cox, C.B. and Dyson, A.E. (1969a) *Fight For Education: A Black Paper 1*, London: Critical Quarterly Society.

Cox, C.B. and Dyson, A.E. (1969b) *The Crisis in Education: Black Paper 2*, London: Critical Quarterly Society.

Dahrendorf, R. (1968) *Essays in the Theory of Society*, London: Routledge & Kegan Paul.

Darling, J. (1978) 'Progressive, traditional and radical: a re-alignment', *Journal of Philosophy of Education*, 12: 157–66.

Delamont, S. (1987) 'The primary teacher 1945–1990: myths and realities', in S. Delamont (ed.) *The Primary School Teacher*, Lewes: Falmer Press.

DES (1978) *Primary Education in England*, London: HMSO.

DES (1982) *Education 5 to 9: An Illustrative Survey of 80 First Schools in England*, London: HMSO.

DES (1988) *Education Reform Act*, London: HMSO.

DES (1988) *Task Group on Assessment and Teaching*, London: HMSO.

Docking, J.W. (1987) *Control and Discipline in Schools: Perspectives and Approaches*, London: Harper & Row.

Donaldson, M. (1978) *Children's Minds*, London: Fontana.

Easen, P. (1985) *Making School-Centred INSET Work*, London: Routledge.

Egan, K. (1983) *Education and Psychology: Plato, Piaget and Scientific Psychology*, London: Methuen.

Engelmann, S. and Carnine, D. (1982) *Theory of Instruction*, New York: Irvington.

Fontana, D. (1981) *Psychology for Teachers*, London: Macmillan.

Fontana, D. (1987) *Classroom Control*, London: Methuen.

Galton, M. (1989) *Teaching in the Primary School*, London: David Fulton.

Georgiades, N.J. and Phillimore, L. (1975) 'The myth of the hero innovator and alternative strategies for organizational change', in C. Kiernan and F. Woodford (eds) *Behaviour Modification for the Severely Retarded*, Amsterdam: Association Scientific.

Gipps, C. (1984) 'Issues in the use of standardized tests by teachers', *Bulletin of the British Psychological Society*, 37: 153–6.

Gluckman, M. (1965) *Politics, Law and Ritual in Tribal Society*, Oxford: Blackwell.

References

Golby, M. (1988) 'Traditions in primary education', in M. Clarkson (ed.) *Emerging Issues in Primary Education*, Lewes: Falmer Press.

Hargreaves, A. (1984) 'Contrastive rhetoric and extremist talk', in A. Hargreaves and P. Woods (eds) *Classrooms and Staffrooms: The Sociology of Teachers and Teaching*, Milton Keynes: Open University Press.

Harlen, W. (1982) 'Matching', in C. Richards (ed.) *New Directions in Primary Education*, Lewes: Falmer Press.

Heritage, J. (1984) *Garfinkel and Ethnomethodology*, Cambridge: Polity Press.

Heritage, J. and Greatbach, D. (1986) 'Generating applause: a study of rhetoric and response at party political conferences', *American Journal of Sociology*, 92, *1*: 110–57.

Hirst, P.H. (1974) *Knowledge and the Curriculum*, London: Routledge & Kegan Paul.

Hughes, M. (1986) *Children and Number: Difficulties in Learning Mathematics*, Oxford: Blackwell.

Jenkins, G. (1976) 'The systems approach', in J. Beishon and G. Peters (eds) *Systems Behaviour*, Milton Keynes: Open University Press.

Kelly, A.V. (1982) *The Curriculum: Theory and Practice*, London: Paul Chapman.

Kelly, A.V. (1988) 'The middle years of schooling', in A. Blyth (ed.) *Informal Primary Education Today*, Lewes: Falmer Press.

Kelly, G. (1977) 'The psychology of the unknown', in D. Bannister (ed.) *New Perspectives in Personal Construct Psychology*, London: Academic Press.

King, R. (1988) 'Informality, ideology and infant's schooling', in A. Blyth (ed.) *Informal Primary Education Today*, Lewes: Falmer Press.

Laing, R.D. (1985) *Wisdom, Madness and Folly: The Making of a Psychiatrist*, London: Macmillan.

Lang, P. (ed.) (1988) *Thinking About ... Personal and Social Education in the Primary School*, Oxford: Blackwell.

Lawton, D. (1980) *The Politics of the School Curriculum*, London: Routledge.

Lawton, D. (1986) 'The curriculum and curriculum change', in A. Cohen and L. Cohen (eds) *Primary Education: A Sourcebook For Teachers*, London: Harper & Row, 142–55.

Lawton, D. and Gordon, P. (1987) *HMI*, London: Routledge.

Leach, P. (1979) *Baby and Child: From Birth to Age Five*, Harmondsworth: Penguin.

Levy, P. and Goldstein, H. (1984) *Tests in Education: A Book of Critical Reviews*, London: Academic Press.

MacDonald, B. (1976) 'Evaluation and the control of education', in D. Tawney (ed.) *Curriculum Evaluation Today: Trends and Implications*, London: Macmillan Education.

Maclure, S. (1988) *Education Reformed*, Sevenoaks: Hodder & Stoughton.

Magee, B. (1987) *The Great Philosophers, an Introduction to Western Philosophy*, London: BBC Books.

Measor, L. (1985) 'Critical incidents in the classroom: identities, choices and careers', in S.J. Ball and I.F. Goodson (eds) *Teachers' Lives and Careers*, Lewes: Falmer Press.

Miller, J. (1983) *States of Mind*, London: BBC Books.

Morrell, F. (1989) *Children of the Future: The Battle for Britain's Schools*, London: Hogarth Press.

Mortimore, P., Sammons, P., Stoll, L., Lewis, D., Russell, E., and Ecob, R. (1987) *School Matters: The Junior Years*, London: Open Books.

Nelson-Jones, R. (1983) *Practical Counselling Skills*, London: Cassell.

Nias, J. (1987) 'Teaching and the self', in *Cambridge Journal of Education*, 17, 3: 178–85.

Nias, J. (1989) *Primary Teachers Talking*, London: Routledge.

Nias, J. and Groundwater-Smith (eds) (1988) *The Enquiring Teacher: Supporting and Sustaining Teacher Research*, Lewes: Falmer Press.

Parlett, M. and Hamilton, D. (1976) 'Evaluation as illumination', in D. Tawney (ed.) *Curriculum Evaluation: Trends and Implications*, London: Macmillan.

Peters, R.S. (1966) *Ethics and Education*, London: Allen & Unwin.

Peters, T. and Waterman, R. (1982) *In Search of Excellence*, New York: Harper & Row.

Pollard, A. (1987) 'Primary school teachers and their colleagues', in S. Delamont (ed.) *The Primary School Teacher*, Lewes: Falmer Press.

Pollard, A. and Tann, S. (1987) *Reflective Teaching in the Primary School*, London: Cassell.

Pope, D. (1983) *The Objectives Model of Curriculum Planning and Evaluation*, London: Council For Educational Technology.

Postman, N. and Weingartner, C. (1969) *Teaching as a subversive Activity*, Harmondsworth: Penguin.

Reid, I. (1988) *The Sociology of Education*, London: Fontana.

Richards, C. (1982) 'Primary education 1974–80', in C. Richards (ed.) *New Directions in Primary Education*, Lewes: Falmer Press.

Richards, C. (1988) 'Primary education in England: an analysis of some recent issues and developments', in M. Clarkson (ed.) *Emerging Issues in Primary Education*, Lewes: Falmer Press.

Robertson, J. (1981) *Effective Classroom Control*, Kent: Hodder & Stoughton.

Rutter, M. (1979) *Fifteen Thousand Hours*, London: Open Books.

Rutter, M. (1983) 'School effects on pupil progress: research findings and policy implications', *Child Development*, 54, 1: 1–29.

Salmon, P. (1988) *Psychology for Teachers: An Alternative Approach*, London: Hutchinson.

Sikes, P. (1985) 'The life cycle of the teacher', in S.J. Ball and I.F. Goodson (eds) *Teachers' Lives and Careers*, Lewes: Falmer Press.

Sikes, P.J., Measor, L., and Woods, P. (1985) *Teacher Careers: Crises and Continuities*, Lewes: Falmer Press.

Simon, B. (1978) *Intelligence, Psychology and Education: A Marxist Critique*, London: Lawrence & Wishart.

Simon, B. (1985) *Does Education Matter?*, London: Lawrence and Wishart.

Simon, B. (1986) 'The primary school revolution: myth or reality?', in A. Cohen and L. Cohen (eds) *Primary Education: A Sourcebook for Teachers*, London: Harper & Row, 2–22.

Simon, B. (1988) *Bending the Rules: The Baker 'Reform' of Education*,

London: Lawrence & Wishart.

Skemp, R.R. (1971) *The Psychology of Learning Mathematics*, Harmondsworth: Penguin.

Skynner, R. and Cleese, J. (1984) *Families and How to Survive Them*, London: Methuen.

Smith, F. (1978) 'The politics of ignorance', in L.J. Chapman and P. Czerniewska (eds) *Reading from Process to Practice*, London: Routledge.

Solity, J.E. (1988) 'Systematic assessment and teaching – in context' in G. Thomas and A. Feiter (eds) *Planning for Special Needs*, Oxford: Blackwell, 186–208.

Solity, J.E. and Bull, S.J. (1987) *Special Needs: Bridging the Curriculum Gap*, Milton Keynes: Open University Press.

Solity, J.E. and Raybould, E.C. (1988) *A Teacher's Guide To Special Needs: A Positive Response to the 1981 Education Act*, Milton Keynes: Open University Press.

Steiner, C.M. (1974) *Scripts People Live*, London: Bantam.

Stenhouse, L. (1975) *An Introduction to Curriculum Research and Development*, London: Heinemann.

Thouless, R. (1974) *Straight and Crooked Thinking*, London: Pan.

Tizard, B., Blachford, P., Burke, J., Farquar, C., and Plewis, I., (1988) *Young Children in School in the Inner City*, London: Lawrence Erlbaum.

Wheldall, K. and Glynn, T. (1988) 'Contingencies in contexts: a behavioural interactionist perspective in education', in *Educational Psychology*, 8, *1/2*: 5–19.

Wheldall, K. and Merrett, F. (1988) 'Which classroom behaviours do primary school teachers say they find most troublesome?' in *Educational Review*, 40, *1*, 13–27.

White, J. (1982) 'The primary teacher as servant of the State', in C. Richards (ed.) *New Directions in Primary Education*, Lewes: Falmer Press.

Wilkinson, A. (1975) *Language and Education*, Oxford: Oxford University Press.

Wittgenstein, L. (1984) *Philosophical Investigations*, Oxford: Blackwell.

Author index

Subject index